Praise for

It has been said that "our children are the living messages we send to a future we will not see." By that definition, our life's message is captured by *The Dad Difference*. It is a critical message to be shared from one generation to the next. Through this practical, insightful, and engaging message, Brian challenges and inspires dads in this must-read book.

DAN CATHY, Chairman and CEO at Chick-fil-A, Inc.

If you are looking for an authentic, fun, encouraging, and hope-giving book on one of the most important assignments in life—being a DAD—then you've found it. My friend Bryan gives us an up close and personal look at how one of the finest men I know, his father, Crawford, is passing on a purposeful and powerful legacy through his children. Buy two copies—one for yourself and another for a friend who may need an arm around the shoulder or a gentle nudge to excel still more as a dad. The next generation is desperate for dads to "step up."

DENNIS RAINEY, cofounder and host of the radio program FamilyLife Today; author of bestselling book *Moments Together for Couples*

My friend Bryan Loritts has gifted us with a practical and inspiring book to help us in the journey of fatherhood. In a world in need of great men to guide their children, *The Dad Difference* is a must read for every father and aspiring father.

LECRAE MOORE, Grammy Award–winning artist

As a first-time expecting father, this book has been invaluable. As someone who lost their father at a very young age, I had very little guidance in becoming a dad. This book has been incredibly helpful in my preparation for fatherhood.

BRANDIN COOKS, Wide Receiver, Los Angeles Rams

The Dad Difference is a gift to men, providing clarity in one of life's most daunting journeys—fatherhood. In clear and compelling language, Bryan Loritts draws us into the Scriptures and his relationship with his own father to show us what every man must pass on to their kids to position them for success. This is a must read.

BENJAMIN WATSON, NFL Veteran

The older I get, the more I realize: you don't know what you don't know. Which is quite humbling as a dad! I'm so grateful for voices like Pastor Loritts. In this book, he shows us how to lift the next generation above our shoulders, as his father did for him. The wisdom in his message will challenge you, as it did me, to be more intentional as we try to send out tried and true arrows into the world.

KYLE KORVER, NBA Veteran

Relationship. Integrity. Teaching. Experiences. I'm not sure there are four better words to describe having Crawford Loritts as a father. The intentionality in which he has pursued his children in these areas has continued into our adult years. I pray this book blesses you as its truths are continuing to bless me.

HEATHER LORITTS, Bryan's sister

"If there's anyone in my family that is capable of capturing such a wonderful and heartfelt tribute of our dad, it would be my brother. In *The Dad Difference*, you will be encouraged, challenged, as well as enlightened by the life of our father, Crawford Loritts Jr. Dad, thank you so much for modeling the desired destination. I love you dearly.

BRYNDAN LORITTS, Bryan's brother

Children are not born with a manual. However, having a godly foundation is comforting during the most difficult parenting seasons. My brother's book lovingly and accurately captures the examples, principles, and high (but attainable) standards of my wonderful father. Dad blessed us with parenting tools and techniques that I both cherish and utilize to this day.

HOLLY L. GIBSON, Bryan's sister

As a father who is about to release his youngest daughter off to college, how I wish that I had had a book like *The Dad Difference* back when I was just starting out. Bryan is wise beyond his years, with great passion and practical wisdom for us parents who wish to be present, intentional, and Christ-centered in the way that we raise our kids. Whether you are an experienced parent, a new parent, or perhaps looking forward to being a parent someday, the insights Bryan shares in these pages are ones you won't want to miss.

SCOTT SAULS, pastor of Christ Presbyterian Church in Nashville, TN, and author of *A Gentle Answer*

Bryan Loritts's newest book, *The Dad Difference*, is both a divine and practical look at being a dad. Why? Because Bryan draws from principally two sources he trusts—the Scriptures and his earthly father, Dr. Crawford Loritts. I have had the amazing privilege and blessing of having Crawford as a good and trusted friend for over thirty years. What I have seen and experienced in Crawford is only a fraction of what Bryan has seen. But what I have grown to know is a man of integrity, with complete trust and faith in the Word of God; cherishing his wife, Karen; loyalty and transparency with his children, friends, and associates; always leaning into and trusting the Holy Spirit. So when Bryan shares four major virtues of a great dad, rest assured, it is based upon watching a man trusting God and His Word, and how that affected the way he fulfilled his role as a dad. The powerful intersection of divine truths and an earthly example!

STEVE ROBINSON, former VP of Marketing for Chick-fil-A

THE DAD DIFFERENCE

THE 4 MOST IMPORTANT GIFTS YOU CAN GIVE TO YOUR KIDS

BRYAN LORITTS

MOODY PUBLISHERS

CHICAGO

Unless otherwise indicated, Scripture quotations are from the ESV® Bible (The Holy Bible, English Standard Version®), copyright © 2001 by Crossway, a publishing ministry of Good News Publishers. Used by permission. All rights reserved.

Scripture quotations marked KJV are taken from the King James Version.

Scripture quotations marked (NIV) are taken from the Holy Bible, New International Version®, NIV®. Copyright © 1973, 1978, 1984, 2011 by Biblica, Inc.™ Used by permission of Zondervan. All rights reserved worldwide. www.zondervan.com. The "NIV" and "New International Version" are trademarks registered in the United States Patent and Trademark Office by Biblica, Inc.™

Published in association with the literary agency of Wolgemuth & Associates.

Edited by Kevin P. Emmert
Interior and cover design: Erik M. Peterson
Cover illustration of father and child copyright © 2019 by Ron and Joey / Shutterstock (131273324). All rights reserved.
Author photo: Alex Ginsburg Photographics

All websites and phone numbers listed herein are accurate at the time of publication but may change in the future or cease to exist. The listing of website references and resources does not imply publisher endorsement of the site's entire contents. Groups and organizations are listed for informational purposes, and listing does not imply publisher endorsement of their activities.

Library of Congress Cataloging-in-Publication Data

Names: Loritts, Bryan C., author.
Title: The dad difference : the 4 most important gifts you can give to your
   kids / Bryan Loritts.
Description: Chicago : Moody Publishers, [2020] | Includes bibliographical
   references. | Summary: "The Dad Difference explores the four gifts every
   kid needs from their dad. Learn what they each mean and how to put them
   into practice. Full of biblical wisdom, simple truths, and practical
   advice, this book will empower you to become a dad who makes a
   difference for your children"-- Provided by publisher.
Identifiers: LCCN 2019059140 (print) | LCCN 2019059141 (ebook) | ISBN
   9780802419620 (paperback) | ISBN 9780802498540 (ebook)
Subjects: LCSH: Fatherhood--Religious aspects--Christianity. |
   Fathers--Religious life.
Classification: LCC BV4529.17 .L675 2020 (print) | LCC BV4529.17 (ebook)
   | DDC 248.8/421--dc23
LC record available at https://lccn.loc.gov/2019059140
LC ebook record available at https://lccn.loc.gov/2019059141

Originally delivered by fleets of horse-drawn wagons, the affordable paperbacks from D. L. Moody's publishing house resourced the church and served everyday people. Now, after more than 125 years of publishing and ministry, Moody Publishers' mission remains the same— even if our delivery systems have changed a bit. For more information on other books (and resources) created from a biblical perspective, go to: www.moodypublishers.com or write to:

Moody Publishers
820 N. LaSalle Boulevard
Chicago, IL 60610

1 3 5 7 9 10 8 6 4 2

Printed in the United States of America

DEDICATION

To "Coach E"—A dad of two, along with all the young men you coach. Your fathering is worthy of mimicry.

CONTENTS

PART 3: TEACHING

PART 4: EXPERIENCES

FOREWORD

For twenty-seven years my wife, Karen, and I served on the staff of Cru (formerly Campus Crusade for Christ). When we joined staff, Bryan was almost five and Heather was not quite a year old. Bryndan and Holly would come along several years later. As they were growing up, I was away from home a lot, speaking on college campuses and at various conferences and events. My heart was torn. I was doing what God called me to do, but I missed my family.

I was haunted by the tragic stories of pastors and Christian leaders whose children didn't want to have anything to do with the ministry because, in their minds, it robbed them of a heart connection with their dad. Certainly, nobody wants this to be their story, and Karen and I didn't want it to be ours. I can't tell you the number of times during those years I would be in a hotel in some college town and wake up in the middle of the night, slip to my knees, and cry out to God, "Please don't let my children be bitter and reject the faith because I am away."

So today when I see our children walking with the Lord, and our sons loving and leading their families and, yes, preaching and teaching God's Word, I am overwhelmed with gratitude to our great God for His mercy and grace. Karen and I are humbled and filled with praise and thanksgiving for what He is doing in and through their lives. Often the tears trickle down our cheeks when we listen to them speak or when we read one of Bryan's books. And my mind goes back to those nights on the road when I pleaded with the Lord to protect their hearts.

To be sure, I was intentional about connecting to the hearts of our children. This in large part is because of the impact my father has had on my life. Next to Jesus Christ, Pop has had the greatest influence on who I am and my commitment to our marriage and to our children. No doubt about it, I was given the gift of a great dad. He not only shaped my life but he gave me a blueprint for what it looks like to be a father. But my dad didn't do it perfectly, and neither did I.

Bryan is our firstborn and was born on my birthday. We share a bit of a special relationship. But I had no idea that he was writing a book about fatherhood and that so much of it would be centered around stories about my impact and influence on his life. As I read the manuscript, I was moved by the depth of his love and respect for me. I was also relieved that he left out some stories that, let's just say, reveal a lot more of my humanity.

But this is not a book about me. It is a book about being a dad, a passion to aspire to be a portrait of the destination for your children. It is a wonderful, compelling resource underscoring the four most important gifts a father can give to his kids. These gifts are relationships, integrity, teaching, and experiences. In Bryan's words, these gifts will produce "tailwind dads," putting wind in the sails of your children. I agree. I am praying that as you journey through these pages your heart will be filled with hope and encouragement. I am praying that the you will embrace your privileged calling to be a dad and that you will take those inevitable setbacks, hit the reset button, and go after it again.

You're not alone. The resources of heaven are at your disposal. Thanks, son, for this tribute and treasure. Love you much!

Dad
(DR. CRAWFORD W. LORITTS JR.)

TAILWIND DADS

Several decades into pastoral ministry, in which I've logged thousands of hours trying to help people sort through their lives, has only strengthened my conviction that *Dad* is the most powerful three-letter word in the English language. And while I can hear some object by calling my attention to another three-letter word, *God*, it cannot be lost on us that how we see the latter is often predicated on what our experience was with the former. For better or for worse, right or wrong, by his absence or presence, Dad's shadow looms large over our lives.

I live on the West Coast and fly a good deal. Many times, I've boarded a plane headed across the country. Having done this enough times, I've learned to count on a tailwind whenever I journey from west to east, which means I get there faster. And, of course, there's the predictable headwind slowing my trek home as I venture from east to west. No matter which direction I travel, pockets of turbulence are inevitable.

Dads, by our actions we will prove to either be a tailwind or a headwind in the lives of our children. No matter how bad your father may have been, you can still get to your destination, but chances are it will take you significantly longer to get there than if you had a great dad. Absent, abusive, or passive fathers are headwinds forcing their children to squander valuable moments of their adulthood undoing what their fathers did or did not do, when dad should have been there inspiring and pushing them to their God-intended destiny.

But show me a great dad—a dad who was present, and had an otherworldly vision for his child and was an active, caring participant in her life—and I will show you a tailwind, setting his child on a trajectory for success and influence for generations to come. I'm not just telling you what I think, but what I know.

To this day, I still feel the effects of my Tailwind Dad. It's uncanny how often I've found myself caught between life's proverbial rock and hard place, only to canvass the halls of my mind searching for examples of what Dad would have done when faced with a similar situation. Korie and I have been married for several decades now, and much of that is because my father has served and loved my mother for almost a half century, leaving me an example worthy of mimicry. Most mornings, I'm up early reading the Bible and praying because that's what I saw my Tailwind Dad doing. And when I needed someone to just process and pray with me during those pockets of turbulence in the journey of life, it was nice to be able to pick up the phone and call Dad. I've achieved more in less time, not because of how smart or lucky I am, but because I had a caring, involved, intentional, godly dad in my life.

However, not everyone has a journey like mine. Tragically, many children will spend significant stretches away from their biological fathers, which means, for most, the journey into adulthood will go from east to west. During most people's journey into adulthood, headwinds are far more common than tailwinds.

You may resonate with the story of one of my closest friends. He was born out of wedlock to a teenage mom and raised by his grandmother. His father was around, but not truly present. He played no active role in his son's life. Steeped in passivity, my friend's father didn't proactively invest in his son. Consequently, my friend was forced to wander aimlessly into adulthood, with no compelling transcendent vision for his life. But to see my friend now, decades and thousands of miles later, is to witness a breathtaking portrait of fatherhood. He is actively involved with his two children, raising them with eternity in mind. He cooks them breakfast, reads to them at night, and memorizes Scripture with them. He's been married to his bride for almost twenty years and models to his family what authentic, caring manhood looks like. At some point, my buddy made the decision to be a tailwind, even though all he experienced with his dad was a headwind.

I don't know what's going on right now with you and the mother of your children. You may be together, separated, or divorced. But none of that really matters when it comes to your childhood or your children. As H.B. Charles Jr. once said, "Your past may explain you, but it doesn't excuse you."[1] You can decide right this moment to be a tailwind in the lives of your children, pushing them to their God-ordained destinies. This is why I write. I'm here to inspire you to join the company of dads who have decided to be forces for good in the lives of their kids. Join me in looking at four things every dad must do if we are going to be a tailwind.

WARRIOR DAD

A friend of mine will someday inherit the family business. He's known this for years. You can imagine how excited he is about what lies ahead. But there's something else. The majority of his actions orbit around this looming reality. Where my friend attended college and earned his MBA was determined solely to prepare him to run the business. And from the moment he came on board as a junior vice president for the company his grandfather founded, you never had to tell him to go to work or give it his all. His looming inheritance has fostered a unique sense of purpose, focus, and intensity. I guess you could say his whole life has been arranged around his inheritance.

I'm assuming the same would be true of us if we were in his shoes. What if we knew that the family business would someday be ours, that what was started a few generations ago would be handed down to us, and our sense of livelihood and well-being would depend on how we stewarded the inheritance? Like my friend, I think our lives would be marked by excitement, purpose, focus, and intensity.

The Bible teaches that children are a heritage from the Lord (Ps. 127:3). The word *heritage* means an inheritance. If we knew our parents were leaving us an inheritance, there would be great anticipation. No one ever thinks inheritance and moans.

I think one of the ideas being conveyed to us when the psalmist connects children with our inheritance is profound joy. It goes without saying there are moments when it's hard to be joyful with our children. As I write, I have three teenaged boys in our home, who, thankfully, are all trending toward independence. One in particular has said to us numerous times how he cannot wait to get out of our house because he finds our rules to be stifling. There have been numerous times when his mother and I have wanted to say, "The feeling is mutual"!

Yet, even though parenting is filled with unpleasant moments as we navigate the so-called terrible twos and troublesome teens, I think the psalmist is conveying that when our kids look back on their tour of duty in our home, the prevailing sentiment they should experience from us is one of joy and excitement. We should be cheering them on as they discover who they are and navigate life. Children are a heritage.

But just as my friend orders his life around his pending inheritance, many dads do the same when they take out life insurance policies, invest in stocks, and maybe even buy land, partly to leave something for their family when they die. The Bible actually says this is the mark of a good man (see Prov. 13:22). But when the psalmist says that children are a heritage, he is saying that, in our investment portfolio, children are the most valuable commodity we have. Sure, money and investments will be what many dads leave and will have some impact on the people they leave them with. But well-fathered children are what will truly mark our world for a time we will not see. Children are the deposits we make into the future.

Imagine an investment guru like Warren Buffett came to you and said, "Do I have a stock tip for you! If you invest in this commodity, watch over it carefully, and are intentional with it, then you are more than likely to shape not just the economy but the world for good." How would you respond? Chances are you would be poised to invest. What Warren Buffett is to the stock market, God is to life and the family—only more. He's the expert, and in this psalm you have God saying that well-fathered and invested-in children are poised to be a force for good for generations to come. God's message is clear when He says children are a heritage. Do everything you can to invest in them.

I think the psalmist is saying every home should be proactive in having children. For some, this is an incredibly sensitive subject, as well it should be. Maybe you have been trying for a long time to have children but your battle with infertility seems to be a losing one. And then there's the married couple who for whatever reason just doesn't want to have children; it's never been a priority. But if I hear the psalmist correctly, when he says the primary way to shape the world is through well-fathered (and -mothered) children, then this should give us pause to at least begetting children or consider adopting, fostering, or mentoring. Children are a heritage.

THE DAD DIFFERENCE

LIKE ARROWS

Right on the heels of saying children are a heritage, the psalmist uses a poignant analogy: "Like arrows in the hand of a warrior are the children of one's youth" (Ps. 127:4). The comparison of children to arrows suggests they are designed to be released toward a particular goal in mind. But sadly, if this psalm were to be rewritten to match what's happening all too often in America today, it may well read, "Like *boomerangs* in the hand of a warrior are the children of one's youth." Instead of being released for good, our children are venturing out only to return.

Many of us are in an age of extended adolescence, wanting the privileges of adulthood without its responsibilities[1] Adolescence, therefore, is more of a mindset than an age, but nevertheless some have observed that adolescence has extended to age thirty-five.

You may never have heard the phrase "extended adolescence," but my guess is you know some who fit this category. They tend to be males in their twenties or thirties who have no real ambition in life. Some live at home, playing video games all day, and show up frequently on social media where they pontificate the problems of the world, all from the comfort of Mom and Dad's home. Others choose to live with their girlfriend but have no intention or desire of getting married and starting a family. Cohabitation fits well with the narrative of extended adolescence as it gives people the privileges of marriage without the responsibilities. Others still have a career and live on their own but don't seek other responsibilities and joys of adulthood.

How did we get here? An Asian friend of mine told me some

time ago that in Asian culture the one word to describe parents' aspirations for their children would be *successful*. He went on to observe that it seems the one word that describes most American parents' ambitions for their children is *happy*. My experience tells me my friend is right.

While it's become quite fashionable to critique the younger generation for the participation trophy everyone received in their four-year-old soccer leagues, we often neglect to ask whose idea it was to give everyone these trophies in the first place. Any misgivings we may have toward the following generations should in some way hold their parents partly responsible, and the evidence points to us parents being complicit in their failure to launch.

The American obsession with happiness has led to another well-known sociological phrase: *helicopter parenting*. This type of parenting strips children of what Angela Duckworth described in her award-winning book, *Grit*. When Dad and Mom always jump in to ensure their son or daughter is never deprived of an ounce of happiness, they limit their children's resiliency, setting them up for long-term struggles.

I love reading biographies. Many biographies are about great people who, for the most part, came from nothing only to struggle until they finally tumbled into greatness. On more than one occasion, I have wondered about their children and why is it rare for any of them to live biography-worthy lives like their parents. My guess is when their parents finally achieved greatness, the first thing they said was that their kids would never have to struggle the way they did, thus handicapping them from the very thing that made them great—struggle.

A friend relayed to me a story that gets to the heart of the problem. A colleague of his was in the midst of an interview with a young man fresh out of grad school when he decided to abruptly end things only ten or so minutes into the interview. Shocked, this young man asked why the interview had ended so soon. In a very matter-of-fact way, the interviewer called his attention to his cellphone, which had been the focus of the interviewee's attention the whole time, as he was reading and responding to text messages. But this is hardly the end of the story. Later on that day, this young man must have talked to his mom, because she reached out to my friend's colleague, letting him know how qualified her son was for the job and appealing to him to reconsider. When she discovered her pleas were getting nowhere, she gave him a piece of her mind and then promptly hung up on him. Oh boy...

Coddling moms and passive dads are what you get when the transcendent value in parenting is your child's happiness. And when this occurs, the results will be boomerang children who may venture out momentarily into the world, but when they discover they are not the center of the world, will return to the one place where they were—home. We need a loftier vision for our children than their personal happiness.

Scholar Ray Vander Laan observes that around the time Psalm 127 was written, Jewish children would typically go to school from about age five until age twelve. While the average Jewish girl was betrothed for marriage between twelve to fourteen, their brothers found themselves like my friend—learning the ropes of the family business, which would one day be their inheritance. And, of course, it was during this period where around the age of thirteen they experienced what we would now call the bar mitzvah. In this communal moment, they were blessed to step into manhood, love God with the totality of their being, work hard, and live beyond themselves. The Jews—and every other ancient society—knew nothing of a seven-year mulligan called adolescence. Taking their cues from God, the Jews expected their children to live with eternity in mind.[2] That's right, the average thirteen-year-old boy in Jewish antiquity was preparing for marriage, working hard all day, studying Scripture, and in certain seasons fighting in war—and by war, I'm not referencing the video game *Call of Duty*.

The Jewish parent, and especially the father, took raising children seriously. They had to. The success of the family business and even their city necessitated well-fathered children. We catch a glimpse of this in our psalm. A casual observation of Psalm 127 reveals the connection between the home and the city. Right after describing children as arrows, the psalmist concludes, "Blessed is the man who fills his quiver with them! He shall not be put to shame when he speaks with his enemies in the gate" (v. 5). Most towns in antiquity did not have the luxury of having an army that people could join at their leisure. If you were a son, you were a part of the army, and it was your duty to protect the city. When the enemy came to attack, they came to the gates of the city where the army—staffed with everyone's son who had been trained by their dads—came to meet the enemy in warfare. The long-term viability of the city was in direct proportion to its being staffed with well-fathered sons who had been trained for warfare by their dads. As goes the home, so goes the city.

We know these sons had been trained by their dads, because in comparing them to arrows, the psalmist says they were in the "hand of a warrior." The masculine metaphor of warrior implies a father. Of course this doesn't mean mothers do not play an essential role in the development of their children. Books could be and have been written on the devastating effects of children who grow up without the nurture and care of mom. Yet notice the one picking up and pointing the arrow toward the target—warrior dad.

Arrows are designed to strike a target, leaving a mark. A skilled archer does not intend to shoot an arrow whimsically or haphazardly. Instead, he aims the arrow with careful intensity and releases it toward a target far away. For an arrow to fulfill its destiny, it must be handled with a vision.

What's the vision you have for your child? You may not have written it down, but you have one. One of the ways you can discern the target you're aiming your child toward is to ask yourself, *What activity do we spend the most time discussing or doing together? Athletics? Academics? Dance? Some other extracurricular activity? God?*

It's fine to encourage your children in the area of academics, athletics, or some other extracurricular activity. In fact, I think it's necessary to spend time and money in the hopes of them stumbling into what God created them to do by way of vocation. I tell my children, "Do what you love, and you'll never work a day in your life." Don't even get me started on the money Korie and I have spent on athletic fees, drum lessons, and the like. But when these things become the ultimate vision for our children, we fail to help them pursue the Bible's vision for their lives.

I tell dads in my church, "Stop acting crazy at your kid's game. Chances are, they're not going pro. I can say this with confidence because they have your genes!" Even worse, let's say it does work out for them, they make it to the top of their field, but along the way their identity has been based on this thing. Well, now we have an idol, and idols always over-promise and under-deliver. What we need is a transcendent vision.

The Bible casts a compelling vision for us parents with our children. Children are given to us to live out the purposes of God in their generation for the glory of God and the good of humanity (see Deut. 6:4–9; Ps. 78:5–8; Acts 13:36). So that work becomes a platform to advance God's good purposes during our specific moment in history. As I told a group of Christian athletes who play in the NFL, "You're a Christian who happens to play football, not a football player who happens to be a Christian."

This vision of parenting demands we aim our arrows (children) toward something completely outside of themselves. We must parent with a transcendent vision. Life is most fulfilling when we live outside of ourselves and into something beyond us. It is counterintuitive, but the way to happiness begins when we stop looking inward. Words like *selfless* and *sacrifice* must be part of the core curriculum we give our children. After all, this is what Jesus taught us.

This book is written to give you a clear strategy with your children for unleashing their full potential so they hit their God-intended destiny. Warrior Dad, what does it look like to let loose on our society well-fathered children who live out the purposes of God for their moment in history? You and I must give our daughters and sons four gifts: **R**elationship. **I**ntegrity. **T**eaching. **E**xperiences. Or to make it simple, this is what it means to parent **RITE**.

To parent **RITE** does not guarantee great, God-fearing kids. So if your children don't turn out exactly as you had hoped, please don't ask for your money back! As my father loves to say, parents tend to take too much credit when their kids turn out "good" and too much blame when they don't. We can't manufacture good or great kids. Yet just like good eating habits make long life possible, so parenting **RITE** enhances the probability that our children will hit the targets God has intended for them. As we set on this journey, I pray we'll learn what God intends for us to be as fathers.

PART 1

RELATIONSHIPS

The first gift a dad must give his children is the gift of relationships. We cannot lead effectively those we are not connected to intimately. Healthy relationships demand presence, grace, and time.

Chapter 1

RECEIPTS FROM DAD

The earliest image I have of my father is not some grandiose recollection. In fact, I don't even know why my mind has chosen to hold on to it, as if it were some rare antique. It's the mid-1970s, and I am in the back seat of our Matador, distracted by my Star Wars action figures. Mama is in the front with a blue polyester outfit on, gazing out of her window—and I promise you she looks exactly the same now as she did on that day some forty years ago. As my auntie would say, "Good black don't crack." I feel the car start to slow down, and my father has turned on his signal, indicating he wants to turn. But there's a problem, the same problem he always encountered when he tried to check the rearview mirror to know whether it was really safe to turn. I look up from my Han Solo figure to catch my dad gently tapping my mother and asking her to tilt her head to the right. Without protest, she obliges, and now with her "Angela Davis" Afro out of the way, Dad looks into the mirror. Our eyes meet. He gives me the same wink he always did, accompanied by a wide smile betraying his imperfect teeth, which years later he would get capped. I smile back and then return to Han.

I've always been baffled by the receipts my mind has chosen to hold on to. Why do I remember that smile, those teeth, that mid-1970s drive, but can't remember a single word during our trip? I see those same teeth a decade later when he gave me "the talk," and yet I don't remember what he said. And when I preached my first sermon—a really bad sermon—his smile was there a few rows back, holding my mother's hand, beaming with pride. When the message was mercifully over, I'm almost positive he gave me some encouraging words, but while the words elude me, his presence never did. Dad was there.

There is not a single page on the mental scrapbook of my childhood where I felt Dad's absence. I see him on the banks of Georgia lakes fishing with me. There he is through rearview mirrors smiling. And he's down the third-base line, just outside the fence, loosened tie and rolled-up sleeves glistening in the southern humidity cheering me on. Dad was there. One can never gift relationship without presence. Dad was present.

The story is told of the time when Henry Brooks went fishing with his father, Charles. (Charles was the grandson of John Adams, our nation's second president.) They spent all day together, and later on that evening they separately chronicled the day's events in their journals. The father vented to his journal how he had spent a day fishing and caught nothing. His son Henry had a different take: "Went fishing with my father today, the most glorious day of my life."[1] What marked Henry the most wasn't the catch of the fish but the time with his dad.

Presence matters. I'm not sure what you believe about God, but in reaching for human words to describe Him, biblical academics point out His omnipresence. I know it's a bit of a clunky word, but it means God is everywhere present. One ancient king understood this. His name was David. Surveying his life, one could wonder how ideal David's home life was. His father didn't even invite him to join his brothers when the town prophet came looking for the next king. We know hardly anything about his mother, and what little we do know raises more questions than answers. In a deeply autobiographical moment, David exhaled how he was "brought forth in iniquity, and in sin did my mother conceive me" (Ps. 51:5). David's home life was far from perfect, maybe like the home you were brought up in; yet through it all David never loses hope. His confidence is unshaken as he talks about a good Father who will fill in the gaps and be a tailwind even as his mother and father forsake him (Ps. 27:10). And in Psalm 139, David speaks of this everywhere-present Father who is active in all phases of our lives—from the womb to the grave.

All of us long for this. I'm not sure where you are when it comes to matters of faith, but I do know this—you long for a dad who is present. I've been on death row (just visiting, by the way), and have had men on the precipice of execution ask whether they could pray with me to David's everywhere-present God. I've heard stories of women who would never describe themselves as remotely religious, and yet when trouble came their way, they reached for God. And I've read of soldiers huddled in bunkers, clutching a crucifix while being shot at. One author had it right when he wrote, "There are no atheists in foxholes."

So why do we pray in the face of tragedy, make the sign of a cross before the athletic contest, or welcome the priest to stand by our loved one's bedside? We want to believe there is a God, and that this God is present and active in our lives. You may even find this hard to read because you are nursing some deep disappointment with God so great you've given up on the notion of Him altogether. It's probably tethered to some moment in your life when you really needed Him. Perhaps you asked Him to heal a loved one, grant you the job, or rescue you from danger. You prayed hard, went to church, even joined a church. Yet nothing. So you threw up your hands and left. Why? Could it be your protestations to at least the idea of God are because you desired Him to be a father, and the essential thing you expect of a father is to be present?

And why does humanity inwardly boo the father who punts on his responsibility to his children and simply walks away? Because we know at the core of our being, to be a good father means we are present. We show up. You don't have to sit in a house of worship to know this.

I don't want to make too big a deal of the order of these four gifts we dads must give to our children, but it isn't lost on me that relationships are first, and not just because it would ruin the acronym if it wasn't. We cannot lead without showing up, being present, and walking in relationship. As I've sat with people suffering from fatherhood wounds over the years, the fountainhead to their frustration was rarely tied to dad's incompetence or lack of money, but to his absence. Showing up is most of the battle.

Maybe we begin by rearranging our schedules to attend what really matters to our kids. And when the event is over, we offer a smile instead of words of correction. Years later, they won't remember the wrong note they played at their recital, or the misstep during their ballet performance. Instead, they will remember whether we showed up.

Growing up in Atlanta with parents from the Northeast brought along its comedic moments, like the annual shutting down of the city due to the half-inch of snow. My parents howled as people made a mad dash for the local Winn-Dixie to stock up on milk, bread, and eggs. I used to wonder—why these items? As a kid, I'd have been far more appreciative if Mom came home with Lucky Charms and Rice Krispy Treats.

One year, however, one storm wasn't so funny, at least to me. I was about eight, and Mama had long exchanged the Afro for a perm, and we had replaced our Matador for an army green Volkswagen. My parents' choice of cars was embarrassing. The Matador was orange, and now an army green car? Okay then. While their choice of car color may have been funny, this storm was not. I'm not sure how many inches we got, but I do know it was something Atlanta hadn't seen in a while—though I'm sure if you're from Chicago or thereabouts, it's still laughable. To make matters worse, Dad was gone, and we couldn't get out of the house; the roads were that bad. You'll have to forgive me if I sound a bit dramatic, but remember this is how my eight-year-old mind saw things. I really did feel as if we weren't going to make it. And my fears only escalated because my hero was in Chicago on business.

The telephone rang, and I could tell by the way Mama was talking that it was Dad. I got excited and looked to her for some kind of cue that he was coming home, like that day—because, if he didn't, we'd starve. I was sure of it. When she finished, she extended the phone as long as the cord would allow. All I could eke out was, "Dad, we need you to come home." Again, I have no idea what else he said. The only receipt I have with me of that conversation is really the only thing that mattered: "I'll be home today." We hung up. Fear was replaced with confidence. No dying that day. Daddy was coming home. And not much later, he was.

Chapter 2

BIG FRED

It's a typical Sunday evening around the Matador era, and there I am, situated on the front row of some southern church. I see my feet lurking just over the front pew, and to my left is a little bag stuffed with crayons and coloring books. Mama was petrified that I'd embarrass Dad while he was preaching since it would be just he and I at church that Sunday. So she equipped me with a sack full of distractions, but I don't need them this day. I never did. When my hero stands to preach, I tilt my head back almost as far as it can go to look up. I hold this position for the next forty-five minutes or so until he is done. In some sense, I continue to hold this position when it comes to Crawford Loritts.

Some months later—and I have no memory of this, just what my mother loves to tell people—when asked what I want for Christmas, I request a microphone. That's right, when every other kid wanted a Tonka truck or Slinky, I asked for a microphone. A psychologist would have a field day with this bit of information, unearthing some nugget of narcissism I'm sure. But it's what I wanted, and thankfully my parents got it. Later that Christmas morning, I took my new gift, grabbed my Dr. Seuss book like I remember my father collecting his Bible, and I laid it flat on our old antique milk can the same way Dad placed his Bible on the podium. Mother says I would bang my chubby little fist on the milk can the same way Dad did on the podium. And my first attempt at preaching was a three-word sermon plagiarized from my father: "It's God! It's God! It's God!" Already, Dad's presence had marked me.

My father is a remarkable man, but not everything about him is worth mimicking. Some of the cracks in Dad's life are more quirks—you know, the kind where you just roll your eyes and say, "That's just Dad being Dad." My father is an intensely impatient man. He inherited this from his father. Pop-Pop, as we called my grandfather, expected his dinner at four thirty every afternoon. Not four thirty-five. Not four thirty-one. Four. Thirty. On those rare moments when my nana missed the deadline, Pop-Pop would press his head into his right hand and gently tap the fingers of his left hand on the table. With each tap, Nana would rush to pull things together. No, my father didn't do that to my mama. Remember, my mother is from Philly, like the hood in Philadelphia, and she didn't play that game. He was lucky if she even cooked. But Dad was really impatient. A round of golf with him felt more like someone had flipped an hourglass during a game of Taboo than simply hanging. And if he said we were leaving to go somewhere at a certain time, you'd better be ready five minutes before or you might get left.

But there were other cracks in my father, cracks that I'm still recovering from today. Dad was present, but he was actually gone too much. He's an incredibly driven man who is committed to preaching the gospel. Because he is so gifted and skilled at what he does, invitations for him to preach took him away from me for long stretches of my childhood. Many years, he was gone at least a third to half of the year. It may seem odd I bring this up within the context of him being present, but parents establish what's normal within the confines of their home, which means I assumed everyone's experience with their father was similar to mine. It wasn't until later on in high school when I realized how abstract my childhood was, which led to periods of anger toward my father, but I'm getting ahead of myself.

Yes, Dad is far from deity, and I need you to feel this. If you don't, you'll find it hard to connect to the mosaic of fatherhood I'm trying to piece together from his life. I did not grow up in a sterile environment led by two saints. I was parented by humans, children of Adam, filled with flaws. In hindsight, Dad's ministry trips had a personality-altering effect on my life that still lingers today.

While Dad has more of a nurturing disposition, my mother does not. Mama grew up in a single-parent home, estranged for all but a few months of her life from her father. Being the oldest, she had to take care of her brothers and navigate the minefield of a dysfunctional and volatile home. Her mother never hugged her or told her she loved her. Early on, Mama learned she had to be tough.

Are you doing the math? A nurturing father gone for long

stretches of time plus a mother (whom I knew loved me intensely) who was not equipped to show affection equals an oldest son who to this day has a hard time emotionally connecting with people. Ask my wife.

When people cry in my office, I feel like I'm being asked to dunk a basketball or play a piece by John Coltrane on the saxophone. I'm lost. I struggle to show empathy—not because I don't want to, but because I don't know how. Thirty years removed from home, and I feel like I'm just really getting to know my father. Oh, and throw into the mix my decision to follow in the same career path of my highly successful and well-known father and, of course, I will get perpetual comparisons to him, with each one sending the message "not good enough."

When it comes to the coin of humanity, lurking beneath the liability face resides amazing assets. Having a dad who was being pulled in many directions outside of our Atlanta home forged traits like resilience and strength while attacking entitlement all at once. At the start of my athletic seasons, Dad would pull out his calendar and mark which games he would be able to attend. A good season meant he could make about half. When I asked for him to come to more, he would often say, "Son, I know, but I work." He would then point out that my athletic fees, cleats, and uniforms were paid because of his commitment to work. What's more is he would connect his job to his calling. Years later, I would discover he was talking more in the line of vocation from the Latin *vocatio*, which means "calling." As a child, I got the message: I was not the center of his world, God was. Along the way, his refusal to be at everything gave me two great gifts: seeing a man work hard to provide for his family, and refusing to make me the center of his world. There was a strength and resilience to my father that he was obsessed with passing on to me. Dad was not going to raise any boomerang children.

This is a good place for me to stop and encourage you that while God is omnipresent, we're not. And I'm not talking literally. There's a big difference between relationally prioritizing our children and making them the center of our world. We want the former, not the latter. So maybe what this means is once a quarter, sitting down with your daughter or son and going over their recital or sports schedules, marking which events you can make. And the ones you can't make, you should tell them why. There's an important work trip, or you're taking their mother out of town. This way your absences are carefully explained and your children feel relationally cared for.

My father once left on a trip to San Francisco, and just as he was about to leave, I asked him to bring me back one of those San Francisco Giants fitted baseball caps. This kind of hat was the in-thing when I was in high school, and sporting one from the Giants would make me the talk of our school. He made no promises, and since Dad seldom brought things home for us from one of his trips, I didn't expect to get the hat. So when he returned a few days later with it, I was surprised. Of course, I wore it the next day, for all of about two periods, when one of the biggest guys in school promptly took it off of my head. Later on that evening, Dad noticed I didn't have my cap and asked me where it was. A bit embarrassed, I told him what happened. What he said next frightened me. Turning to my mother, he said,

"Karen, I went out of my way to get Bryan this hat. Don't let him back in the house until he returns with it." Then, looking at me with a firm look, showing no teeth, he said, "I don't care what you have to do to get it back." Talk about a hard choice. Confront Big Fred or be homeless. Mustering up all the courage I could, and coupled with some prayer, I walked into school the next day and politely asked Big Fred for my hat. When I came home, Dad was reading the paper on the sofa. He looked at my head, saw the hat, and continued reading.

Dad's lesson was pretty clear. He refused to solve all of my problems. Sometimes, he would just back us into a corner and say, "Figure it out." These moments were huge for me. Years later, when I would venture out to start a church, raise money, and lead a family, I would hit these "Big Fred" challenges and would have to reach down into a reservoir of resilience and strength, first forged by a father who refused to coddle me. He was present, but he didn't hover.

Your kids are likely a lot more resilient than you give them credit for. Demanding they get a job, telling them to stand up to bullies, or refusing to buy them the latest fashions are much more beneficial for their long-term development as arrows than coddling or hovering over them in your quest to make them happy.

Oh, and if you're wondering how I got the cap back from Big Fred. No, he didn't give it to me when I asked. And I didn't hit him or pay him to give me the cap. I told on him.

Chapter 3

GRACE AT THE
MEAT AND THREE

Relationships are a joint venture between two very flawed individuals, or what the Christian worldview would call sinners. To the Western mind, sin is seen almost solely from an individualistic perspective, but God has a different take. When Adam and Eve sinned, their first movement was both away from God and each other. When the two first got married, they were naked and unashamed, which means they were enjoying comprehensive transparency and vulnerability. But then sin walked into the marriage and changed everything. The first couple replaced transparency and vulnerability with fig leaves. And their daily walk with God was removed altogether from their calendar. Ancient Eastern communities understood exactly the message

Genesis 3 was conveying—sin is social, it tears at the fabric of relationships. Their Father, God, could have killed them for their defiance. Instead, He saved and redeemed their relationship with the water supply of grace.

I smile when I hear women say they don't do well in relationships with other women, finding too much drama in their sisters. If I had the courage, I'd tell them what they're diagnosing in other women is probably true of them as well. Or to hear men moan over how difficult it is to have rich, deep friendships with other men, a type of brotherhood that supersedes mere posturing over whose career is better, is also ironic. If we find friendships with other men difficult, it's probably because we, too, are difficult. Intimacy is hard because sin is so pervasive. We all carry our own set of fig leaves. If, then, there is to be any hope of relationships that flourish over the long haul, we better carry large vats of grace. This is true not only among peers, but of parents toward their children.

My father would not let me take my cherry red Honda Civic to college my first year. He wanted me to get acclimated to my new school and focus on the books. So you can imagine how excited I was when I packed up my little hatchback in the fall of 1992, poised to make the long trip up north to Philadelphia for the start of my sophomore year. Right before I left, Dad reached into his pocket and gave me a gold American Express credit card. I couldn't believe my eyes. It had my name on it, even! Immediately, I began to fantasize about all the stuff I would do with this credit card. There were those jeans I'd wanted from Structure, and that suit from JR Riggings. Plus, I could up my dating game.

No more taking a young lady out for cheap Chinese. I could now afford The Ground Round.

Sensing my thoughts, my father began to flow in the prophetic. Still holding on to the card, he laid out the rules. The card was to be used only for emergencies. "Say it with me, Son," and then for full effect he mouthed slowly, "E-MER-GEN-CIES." Blame it on him being a preacher, because next he felt the need to spell out what constituted an emergency: If my car broke down, pull out the card. If I got a flat tire, put it on the card. He would even allow me to put oil changes or tune-ups on the credit card. Then, he gave me some clear examples of what did *not* count as an emergency: "This is not to fund your love life, clothing desires, or off-campus dining. Got it?" I nodded. Somewhat sobered by all this, I asked an obvious question: "But, Dad, I have a part-time job working in the kitchen. How am I going to pay for this credit card?" He flashed those teeth and informed me that while the credit card had my name on it, it was on his account. Having my name allowed me to make purchases, but I would never get the bill. The bill always came to him, which he would gladly pay in full.

Off I went. For the next several months, things were going well until, well, I lost my mind. My shiny new American Express Gold Card bought me those new clothes, funded a few dates, and footed the bill for the boys trip down to Baltimore. Someone once said all sin is temporary insanity. Yep, that's about right. As they say down South, "My cheese had slid off its cracker," and some weeks later, I got a call from my father who was in Chicago preaching. Mother had informed him of my insanity, my seven-hundred-and-something-dollar insanity, and he was none too pleased. While Dad didn't curse, he did give me an earful. Toward the end, he said something about me having to pay him back every cent, no exceptions. Every. Cent. The only two words I said came right when we hung up the phone: "Yes, sir." Boy, had I worked myself into a jam.

My schedule was already stretched between work and academics, and then when you consider my few-dollars-an-hour dishwashing gig, compared to the enormous bill, there was just no way I was going to be able to pay this within the billing cycle. Account for a little thing called interest, and you can see how deep this hole was going to get. I had no other choice but to get another job down the street at the local mall. The next few weeks were as insane as my spending spree. I took on extra shifts washing dishes. And when one of my coworkers at the mall needed to get out of work, I jumped at the chance to replace him. It was an exhausting stretch. I don't even remember sleeping. Finally, I had the money and mailed the check to dad.

A few weeks later, spring break came, and I took the long drive home to Atlanta. I was apprehensive as Dad and I sat down at the local Meat and Three to catch up. This was the first time we'd seen each other since the credit card incident, and I felt like a failure. We had made an agreement, and I'd violated it. And to make matters worse, here I was preparing for a life of vocational ministry and had fumbled in the character department. But sitting with Dad over lunch, I didn't feel any of that. He flashed those not-yet-capped teeth the way he did when I was in the back of the Matador. He laughed as he told me stories of the latest haps with my siblings, and asked about everything going on in my life *but* the credit card bill. I was thrown by his genuine concern and camaraderie. He didn't feel like a dad. He was starting to feel like a friend whose companionship I did not deserve.

Finally, the bill came and he took out his American Express to pay. Well, that did it. I couldn't take this anymore. "Okay, Dad, when are you going to talk to me about the bill?" Rising from the table he said, "We already did when I called you from Chicago." I'm still confused at this point because you need to know my father is the king of resolution. He'd always revisit some epic mistake to make sure we got the lesson. He'd even preach an impromptu, unsolicited sermon to solidify his point. But there was none of that now. Not content with my shock, he said in a flippant way as we were leaving, "Oh, and I'm sure you know this by now: I never cashed your check." What?

Grace. I had amassed a debt with my father. In his justice and anger, he let me know how disappointed he was. In the end, he paid the bill. A relationship restored. Years after our "Meat and Three," when I had graduated and started my own family, I asked Dad why he never cashed my check. "There was no way I was going to let a credit card bill get in between our relationship."

The irony of grace is that it demands a standard in order to exist. Think about it—in order to extend grace, something someone does not deserve, the object of grace had to have been called to a standard and failed miserably along the way. Dads who make a positive difference in the life of their children call and inspire them to a standard. When my dad gave me the credit card and pointed toward a standard, he did so with my long-range growth and maturity in mind. He knew how important financial steward-ship and accountability were, and he also knew I was nineteen and was probably going to do what most nineteen-year-olds do, if you know what I mean. And when I lost my mind, grace stepped in.

Our children are a reason God extends grace. You're a reason God extends grace. Grace demands failure to exist. And to be human is to guarantee moments of failure. Like the rebellious son in Luke 15 who spoke disrespectfully to his dad, and liter-ally took the money and ran, only to return years later having experienced the agony of defeat, so our children are destined to do stupid things with credit cards, automobiles, cellphones, computers, and extra time—to name only a few. May our grace toward them be as sure as their failure, as sure as the dad who ran down the road with open arms to embrace his rebellious child. As sure as my dad over lunch at the local Meat and Three.

Chapter 4

EPIPHANIES

Heroes need grace too. Mark Twain once quipped that when he was fourteen his father was the biggest fool he'd known, but by twenty-one, he was astonished at how much his old man had learned in seven years. Every child has this epiphany, and yet I seemed to have almost the opposite experience. While I still found myself regaling classmates of the mythological qualities my dad possessed when I was fourteen, it was only a few years later when the scales of his infallibility began to fall from my eyes.

This plunge from hero to human was bound to happen, as it does for every son or daughter. My mother birthed me when she was twenty-two and my father was twenty-three. Pair that with me being the oldest, and it's easy to see how my parents made tons of rookie mistakes on me. Right when my youngest sibling was leaving home for college is when my father said he was just starting to figure this whole parenting thing out. By that time, I was twenty-nine years old, and in *my* rookie season of parenting.

Oldest children have an uncanny habit of comparing notes, leaving us with a pervasive sense of feeling cheated. Have you not read the famous story Jesus tells of two brothers? One leaves home in a fit of irresponsibility, insulting his father by demanding his share of the inheritance prematurely. To the astonishment of his watching brother, the father acquiesces and waves goodbye as the son heads out for what would amount to be a prolonged season of debauchery and waste. Finally, having exhausted both his money and morality, he comes crawling home, begging his father to be hired as a servant, so he could eke out some kind of existence.

Taking in the scene of his rebellious sibling, the older brother shakes his head and sucks his teeth, but what he witnesses next makes him mad. Instead of berating or hiring his youngest son, the father throws him a party, breaking out the best. Seething and unable to contain himself, the older brother reminds the father that while his sibling had been negligent, he had been dutiful. And what has his duty earned him? Nothing. His father had failed him.

Maybe *disappointed* is a better word. Disappointment happens when our real-time experiences are out of alignment with our expectations. Every dad, no matter how good he is, will disappoint his children. You can be on an amazing family devo streak where you are praying and exploring Scriptures with your kids. You may be showing up to all the games, having epic family vacations, and speaking their love languages consistently. But you are a human who will mess up. Sure, what Jesus is getting at in His story is not some mistake or error on the part of the father, but nonetheless there was disappointment.

I don't know to what extent your father disappointed you, but I do know he did. Maybe it was because of some younger-brother fit of immorality on his part. You expected a stable home, but got divorce due to dad's infidelity. Or maybe it was because of some addiction that brought your hero to his knees. Or maybe you really needed him at a moment in your life, and he didn't show up. It's an immutable fact of life—dads disappoint, no matter how good they are.

In another famous Twainism, the renowned author once remarked how youth is a gift wasted on the young. While this may be true for the younger brother, it's definitely not the case for the older. In fact, I'm not sure he even had a youth. I wouldn't be surprised if this older son became so duty driven because of the pressure his parents placed on him. As the one who would soon take over the family business, he was probably pressured daily to get it right and not screw up. And so he became achievement oriented. Then along came his younger brother, and maybe his parents looked out and decided to relax a bit. They've chosen to autocorrect, realizing some things are more valuable than performance—things like relationship, love, and communication. So they give more margin and don't completely freak out the way they used to with their firstborn. But the damage has been done, the trajectory set. The older brother is seeing this and from his perch all he notices is two sets of standards. When maybe if he looked at it from the parents' perspective, they're trying to repent. Who knows.

Did Crawford Loritts Jr. disappoint me? Of course. Looking back, there were times he seemed to parent me with a nervous twitch, shrinking the margin for error on me, their firstborn, to an almost impossible standard. And, of course, there were moments as I watched him throw his suitcase in the car to go catch an airplane when I felt as if ministry was more important than me.

And I've only scratched the surface of his humanity.

John Piper once observed how preaching makes hypocrites out of every preacher. Of course it does. Those who preach pronounce an unattainable standard, too high even for the preacher. And yet Piper would have also been right to exchange the word *preaching* for *parenting*. Yes, it's true, parenting makes hypocrites of us all. No parent fully lives up to the ideals they seek to instill in their children.

I've tried to teach my kids kindness, while at times displaying fits of meanness. And there have been so many times when I've lectured them on the importance of sharing, when I've been selfish, withholding valuable things they desperately need from me like my time and presence.

For the last several years, Delta has awarded me Diamond status, which is their top level for frequent fliers. Every time the gate agent scans my boarding pass and thanks me for my status, I want to tell them it's not as great as you think. Just ask my family.

My itinerate schedule tends to work about eighteen months in advance, as invitations come in for me to speak at various events. Sometimes this creates tension at home, as my children's schedules tend to come into view at a much more immediate pace. So when my wife tells me our middle son Myles's eighth-grade graduation conflicts with a speaking engagement I had on the books for somewhere back East, I feel somewhat conflicted.

I've sat in his kindergarten graduation, and sixth-grade graduation from his school when we lived in Memphis. And now, two years later, there's an eighth-grade graduation, after I've already gone to the sixth-grade one? Plus, I didn't grow up in an era when there were eighth-grade graduations. You know what they did to eighth graders in my small Georgia town? They put us in high school and called us "Sub-freshmen"! Oh, and the hazing was legendary. I can still see my friend's legs poking out of the grey high school garbage can where some junior had stuffed him in butt first. So when I hear of my son's eighth-grade graduation, I respond with the same sort of distracted excitement I do when I'm in a rush for church and my bride asks me what I think of her outfit: "That's great."

I checked in with Myles to gauge how he felt. Would it be okay for me to go, or did he want me to stay for his graduation? He shrugged his shoulders in his typical fourteen-year-old nonchalant way and green-lighted me to go. So I went, and felt uneasy the whole time. Somewhere over the Rockies, I knew I had made a mistake. A big one. My regret deepened when Korie texted me pics of just her and Myles at the graduation. And can you believe she Instagrammed these pics of just the two of them? I knew I had screwed up. When I returned, I went straight to Myles's room where he was sitting on his bed under the watchful eye of his Pink Floyd poster. I asked Myles to forgive me, and with a smile on his face he gave me grace, the same way Dad had given me grace years before at the Meat and Three. He asked for no explanations.

He just simply extended to me what I did not deserve and asked when we were playing golf again. Had he asked to play that day at Pebble Beach, I would have tried to make it happen.

It's taken parenting to teach me that my parents need grace too. I try my absolute best to provide and prepare my children for a life of "good success" (Josh. 1:8–9), but I still come up short. If I have any hopes of a flourishing relationship with my children well into their adult years, I must be quick to extend them grace, and they too must reciprocate the same grace toward me. And my father needs the same grace from me. In human relationships, grace is always a two way street.

Okay, so your dad was anything but a tailwind in your life. His failure has been your pain, a pain that still lingers. Maybe your view of your dad is more of an enemy than a headwind. He wronged you and didn't give you what was yours by right.

Toward the middle of Jesus' famed Sermon on the Mount, He begins to poke and prod in those very sensitive places of our lives, like how we respond to people who have wronged us. Jesus says offensive things, like how we should turn the other cheek, give to those who are trying to sue us, and even go beyond the call of duty with those who have wronged us by carrying their pack an extra mile (Matt. 5:39–41). And then He sums up by exhorting us to love our enemies (5:44). Why should we do these hard—no, impossible—things? Because, Jesus says, speaking of God, "For he makes his sun rise on the evil and on the good, and sends rain on the just and on the unjust" (5:45). Do you know what Jesus is saying? He doesn't just care about the wronged; He also cares about those who have done the wrong. God makes His sun to rise on the lynched and the lynch mob, on the aspiring actress, and the sexually aggressive movie producer who seeks to take advantage of her. God sends the rain on abandoned children, and on abandoning dads. This is so hard to take in.

Okay, maybe a relationship with your dad is out of the question due to him not being apologetic or repentant. I get that. It takes two to have a healthy relationship (see Rom. 12:18). But your dad needs grace. When we give those who wronged us grace, Jesus says we look like our Heavenly Father (Matt. 5:45). When we refuse to return evil for evil, and instead bless those who have wronged us by dispensing grace on their undeserving plates, Jesus essentially says, "Now you look like your Daddy."

But there's another reason for grace; let's call this more of a side effect of grace. It's been said that hurt people hurt people. When we hold on to the pain inflicted on us by our headwind dads, the toxicity of bitterness clogs our hearts and inflicts our spirits. The best thing we can ever do to regain our joy and clear our arteries is to insert the stint of grace, and allow that grace to flow freely and quickly to those who have hurt us.

If we look close enough, every dad—headwind and tailwind alike—has messed up and needs grace, because every dad is flawed. And one day, your children will likewise have an epiphany, when they watch your demise from hero to human, and when that day comes you will likewise need grace.

Chapter 5

LETTERS

Time is the most valuable resource we have, more precious than money. This is a point Peter Drucker makes in his classic, *The Effective Executive*: "The supply of time is totally inelastic. No matter how high the demand, the supply will not go up. There is no price for it and no marginal utility curve for it. Moreover, time is totally perishable and cannot be stored. Yesterday's time is gone forever and will never come back. Time is, therefore, always in exceedingly short supply."[1] Ain't that the truth. Yes, Peter, while we can grow money, we can never grow time. Once the sun sets on today, it's a day we will never get back.

They're rare but treasured moments for me, now. Around once every two years or so, I'll find myself preaching, look out, and there's Dad in the audience, as he was the other day. It bothers me to no end that I've never grown comfortable preaching in front of him, even though I've been doing it now for almost thirty years. The pull on a son to please his dad is overwhelming, and I'm not sure it will ever go away (or that I want it to). But what makes it especially challenging for me now is, often when I see Dad in the audience as I'm preaching, he's wiping tears from his eyes.

My father is aging, and his weathered skin bears the marks of Adam's sin. Sure, the teeth are nice and capped, but the hair is gone, the gait is slowing, and his hearing is not as it once was. Like everyone else fortunate to live well into the fourth quarter of their lives, the old man knows the end is drawing near. His ever growing acquaintance with mortality is the reason for the tears. Time with his family is running out, and he wants to make the most of it.

One of the first times I remember seeing my father cry happened during the late summer of 1991. We had waved goodbye to my Honda Civic, and packed our burgundy Ford Aerostar for the long trek up to Philadelphia, where I would attend college. When we arrived on campus, Mama busied herself making my bed and preparing my dorm room—things she never did for me while I was living at home—against my eighteen-year-old protestations. I was too young to know this was a sobering moment for her—it was more about Mama trying to be a mama in the traditional sense one last time than actually doing chores. And, of course, Dad was stopped a million times by people who recognized him, wanting to reminisce over the sermon he preached years ago that changed their lives. But in a break from his character, Dad was distracted.

Finally, it was time to part ways. Like a couple trying to figure out how to say goodbye after their first date, the moment was awkward. We had just walked out of the registrar's office and were facing the pond that separated the campus from the surrounding neighborhood. Dad was having a hard time looking at me as the family car with my mother and siblings idled a few feet away. Just then, a tear fell from his eyes as he pulled out a letter with my name on it, and pressed it into my hand. "Son," he said, "obey God." And after giving me a warm hug, he walked to the van, and I stood and watched as the Aerostar disappeared.

This was a defining moment in my life. Yes, youth is a gift wasted on the young, because the young do not grasp the fleeting nature of time. But this, this was one of those rare moments when, in my youth, the earth seemed to stand still, and the weight of being far from home, in a place with no friends, and a mind filled with infinitely more questions than answers, bore down on me. What would become of me? Would I get married? To whom would I marry? And, most importantly, did I have what it takes to be the measure of a man my father was?

These questions loomed large in my mind as I found myself walking around the pond, tears dampening my face. When I reached a bench overlooking the pond, I collapsed into it, and pulled out my father's letter—his parting words to me:

Son,

On February 11, 1973 you came into the world, and from the moment we knew you were coming I have always prayed for you. Not a single day of your life has elapsed without me praying for you. The first words you ever heard me whisper into your ears were these: "This book of the law shall not depart from your mouth, but you shall meditate on it day and night, so that you may be careful to do according to all that is written in it. For then you will make your way prosperous, and then you will have good success. Have I not commanded you? Be strong and courageous. Do not be frightened, and do not be dismayed, for the LORD your God is with you wherever you go" (Joshua 1:8–9).

Bryan, the same God who has guided me and your mother these twenty years, will be the same God who will guide you. Obey God! Be strong and courageous!

All my love,

Dad

Over the next four years (and beyond), these letters would become a habit, as I would reach for them in my campus mailbox. Late at night I would sit with them in the corner of some secluded place, the way friends do when they need to share private matters, free from distractions. Dad would write me from London; Cedar Falls, Iowa; Chicago; Atlanta; Zimbabwe; you name it. His letters came with stunning frequency, at least once a week, if not more. His epistles would span everything from where he was and what he was doing to inquisitions into my well-being that didn't feel intrusive. I could tell he missed me and was doing everything he could to keep connected, which I liked. He would also give some sort of earthy advice about my studies, women, money, walk with God, or whatever.

I don't know exactly how Timothy felt when the courier delivered what would be his father figure's final documented letter (2 Tim.), but I imagine there was a sense of pride. Of all the people Paul could have written while in jail—the churches that needed encouragement, the disputes that needed to be navigated—the fact he wrote his "son in the faith" had to have steeled Timothy with great confidence and value.

Time and presence are not always synonymous. Paul could not physically get to Timothy due to his incarceration. Given the sheer practicalities of life, along with the demands of work, my father could not move into the dorm with me. But for more than four years, he spent time with me through his letters.

When my Pop-Pop died, my father was undone. This was his hero, the man who taught him how to fish and introduced him to baseball. They sat together on many a Saturday afternoon at Yankee Stadium watching the likes of Mickey Mantle and Elston Howard play ball. And just like that, he was gone. Not long after my grandfather's death, I walked into Dad's bathroom where I noticed an unusual sight—a bottle of Old Spice cologne. Dad never wore this before, but Pop-Pop did. A whiff of the cheap cologne reminded Dad of his dad. Even Dad needed to be reminded of his dad's presence.

Sometime later, I checked in on my dad, and asked how he was doing. After a considerable pause, and in great restraint, Dad said, "Without thinking, I started to call the old man the other day, and then it dawned on me—he's gone. I miss him." And it dawned on me—children, no matter how hold they may be, always need to hear from Dad.

I'm starting the third quarter of my life—God is so kind—and I still need to hear from my father. Seeing his name light up on my smartphone induces a smile. The text message of him checking in encourages me. And while I don't always take advantage of it, the fact that he's still around and available for any advice I need gives me a kind of security my financial planner can't compete with.

Dads, our children need our presence. Yes, the relationship may be so strained that offering any kind of unsolicited advice or admonishment may be out of bounds, but to offer a call, or a note, to encourage are irreducible minimums every child, no matter what his or her age, needs. When we die, may our children buy a bottle of our most used cologne, because our presence was that pervasive in their lives.

When each of my sons turns eleven, my father goes out and buys a brand-new Bible and engraves their name on it. Over the next two years, my dad will prepare sermons, scribble notes, and preach out of this Bible. He will also use it for his personal time with the Lord, reading it from end to end—and along the way, he will write prayers in the Bible for this particular grandson. Then, when his grandson turns thirteen, he flies out for a rite-of-passage celebration. There's shopping, great food, and lots of laughter. Then, in a quiet moment, Dad will stand, pull out the Bible he's been working through the previous two years, and turn to the front page where he has written a prayer for his grandson.

In addition to some direct personal challenges, the prayer also contains a historical recounting of the faithfulness of God to the Loritts family, along with a challenge to continue the legacy of Jesus loving black men, a legacy that began with their great, great, great grandfather who was a praying slave. It will also contain the words of Joshua 1:8–9, the very first words my sons heard their grandfather, the patriarch of the family, whisper into their ears, calling them to courage. As these words are being read, I can see the confidence swelling in my boys' souls. Without fail, they wake up early the next day, unprompted by anyone, pull out their new Bible, and read God's Word. Dad's letters are inspiring another generation of Loritts men.

Encouraging words are the jet stream propelling your children toward their God-ordained targets. It's not just the tongue that wields the power of life and death; the pen is powerful too. Write the letter, send the text, type the email, and inspire your children to courage, no matter how old they may be. While they may have left your home, it's not too late to encourage.

PART 2

INTEGRITY

Great fathers give their kids the gift of integrity.
More than listening to what we say, our children
will watch what we do. When actions and words
become one, we call that integrity.

Chapter 6

WHEATIES

My father never made a promise to me he did not keep. The more I think about it, Dad didn't make too many promises. His word was so good, phrases like "You can trust me," "I promise you," or "I'm serious this time," were unnecessary. If Dad said it, he did it. Crawford Loritts is a man of integrity.

But what exactly does *integrity* mean? If I had to define the term, I would say *integrity* is the alignment of words with deeds. Or, to say it more succinctly, *integrity* means we do what we say. Transformative leadership happens when a person embodies the ideals and values they seek to pass on to those who follow them. While integrity may seem to mean less and less in certain sectors of our society, in our homes it's a matter of life and death.

The apostle Paul knew nothing of a leadership divorced from integrity. In fact, in his spiritual fathering of Timothy, he extended bold invitations for Timothy to not just heed his sermons or letters, but to actually follow how he lived: "You, however, have followed my teaching, *my conduct*, my aim in life, my faith, my patience, my love, my steadfastness" (2 Tim. 3:10, emphasis added). Earlier in the letter, Paul exhorted Timothy to share in suffering for Christ (1:8). How could Timothy take on such a bold challenge? Paul answers a few verses later: "Which is why I suffer as I do" (1:12). Paul could exhort Timothy to suffer because he himself was personally invested. We call that integrity.

I once heard of a well-known professor, who, when he died, had a private gathering of some of his former students convened at his home to pay their respects. This professor had spent all of his years challenging his students to lead from integrity, so the room was surprised when one of the guests said that, while a student, he was asked to babysit this professor's children. He confessed how, later on that evening, he ventured into his beloved professor's study, saw his checkbook on the desk, and started to thumb through it. His colleagues were stunned by the admission. And then he remarked how, after looking at his professor's deposits and expenses, he was shocked on two fronts: how little he made and how much he gave.

Growing up in Atlanta back in the eighties had its challenges, especially if you were a sports fan. I didn't have too many heroes to look up to when it came to my favorite football team, the Atlanta Falcons. So I set my gaze on the Chicago Bears and their star running back, Walter Payton, or "Sweetness," as he was called. I loved Walter Payton. I loved him so much, I did the unthinkable—I ate Wheaties. If you've never had Wheaties, consider yourself fortunate. Wheaties is, in my opinion, the worst cereal ever. I so wanted to be like Walter Payton. I figured since he was on the cover of the Wheaties box that he actually ate them. And if "Sweetness" ate Wheaties, then I'd eat them too. Like Paul's invitation to Timothy, I was following Walter Payton's *conduct*—or so I thought.

From time to time, professional teams would ask my dad to preach at their chapel service. Well, as God would have it, one day the Bears were in town to play the Falcons and asked my father to speak. When he asked me if I wanted to go, I sarcastically looked at him like Arnold looked at his dad on the hit eighties show *Diff'rent Strokes*. Dad got the message, and a few days later we headed down the freeway to see my other hero.

It's hard to imagine things could get much better than sitting in the same room as Walter Payton listening to my father preach. But after the service ended, they did. The chaplain invited us to stay for breakfast with the team, which we naturally accepted. And my mind was blown when we were seated at the same table as Walter Payton!

I was freaking out, barely able to contain myself. Yet it's what I saw next that disturbed me, because my hero was not eating Wheaties. He was eating Raisin Bran. My nine-year-old mind was working overtime. *No. He. Didn't. Here I am, making all these sacrifices, taking up my cross and the whole nine by eating Wheaties, and you're eating Raisin Bran? I need an explanation.* So, mustering up all the courage and respect I could, I gently told Mr. "Sweetness" how I eat Wheaties because he eats Wheaties, and then why is he not eating Wheaties now? After a moment of laughter, he said how he never eats Wheaties because he hates the taste of them. He much preferred to eat Raisin Bran.

I never ate Wheaties again.

At the time, I knew nothing of marketing, brand management, and endorsement deals. Had I known, I would have quickly understood what was going on with my hero. All Wheaties was to him was a paycheck and an opportunity to extend his brand. My deep disappointment stemmed from the epiphany that he was not even buying what he was selling. Publicly he communicated one thing, but when the lights and cameras were off, Raisin Bran it was.

Life is filled with challenges. We live in a broken world where opportunities to cheat, cut corners, and compromise our moral convictions abound. Too many dads pose as if they're eating their Wheaties, when in reality they're eating Raisin Bran, and the effects are devastating.

I was hanging out with some pastor friends of mine, and we were talking about this idea of integrity—and specifically the kind of sexual integrity men need to have within marriage. The conversation turned to the depths of devastation that sexual infidelity among pastors inflicts on the congregation. Why is this? One friend offered a guess: For most men, the only man they have consistent contact with who represents moral integrity is their pastor—their spiritual father. What they're used to is a fraternity of men secretly bingeing on Raisin Bran.

Our kids need dads who will eat their Wheaties. I think you get my point. Our world is populated with enough people who have become public successes but private failures. It's easy to project one image on social media, but when it is just us with our children they see us eating Raisin Bran. We need dads who will honor their wives in public and behind closed doors. Dads, we need you to not just lecture your children on the evils of pornography, but to fight the good fight yourself. And may our word be so good we don't need to say things like "I promise," "I'm serious this time," or "You can trust me." Let's eat our Wheaties.

Chapter 7

APOLOGIES

So what happens when we don't eat our Wheaties? Not *if* we don't, but *when* we don't? If you're human, you've messed up. You know what it's like to have the best of intentions, but you failed. Every mistake is a breach of integrity, a tearing asunder of our deeds from our words.

My father is a flawed hero. It's a bit of an oxymoron, but it's so true. Dad is a man of integrity who has disappointed me and my siblings over the years.

Dad tended to parent me, the oldest child, like a patient sitting in the waiting room on the precipice of surgery. He was a bit jumpy, nervous I had blown it—which I did more than I'd like to admit. So he tended to come down on me pretty hard at times and could've used some more helpings of patience.

THE DAD DIFFERENCE

One of my chores growing up was cutting the grass. I hated to cut the grass. Who am I kidding? I *hate* cutting the grass. Combine the humidity of Georgia with our house sitting on a steep incline, and you can see how I would procrastinate when it came to this chore. So Dad was constantly on me about doing it.

I once remember coming home from college, a big-time freshman, when Dad told me to cut the grass. I curtly responded, "I don't do grass," to which he replied, "Do you do tuition?" A few minutes later, I cranked up the old lawn mower.

In the middle of Dad's growing frustration, feeling as if I was blowing him off with the whole grass thing, he left for another trip. On his way out the door, he made it clear that when he came back a few days later, he expected the grass cut, no exceptions. When his plane touched down seventy-two hours or so later, the grass had not been cut. It was summertime, and I was sitting in the front room watching an episode of *Fresh Prince*, when I heard him pull up. By the way his car door closed I could tell he was not pleased. Shortly after the door opened, he laid into me pretty good, emphatically stating his disappointment, demanding I turn the television off, and grounding me for a few weeks. All of this happened within the span of seventy-five seconds, and without me being able to respond. Like a child trying to get in a game of Double Dutch, my mother kept trying to interject, but Dad wasn't hearing it. Finally, when his homily was over, Mama explained how it had rained nonstop all while he was gone. Dad's countenance changed, and he picked up his bags and headed straight for his bedroom, where moments later he emerged dressed in shorts, a T-shirt, and a hat, and left the house. We all knew where he was headed, and he wasn't leaving to cut the grass—unfortunately. Dad was going on a prayer walk.

My father is a man of prayer. His normal mode of prayer was on his knees, or out at the local coffee shop writing his prayers in his journal. Prayer walks were another thing altogether. He tended to do these when he was especially upset at something we had done. If we lied, he went on a prayer walk. If we were disrespectful to Mama, he went on a prayer walk. If we stole something, you guessed it, a prayer walk. While Dad was talking to God around our little neighborhood, an anxious stillness would come over our home as we awaited his reentry. After a while, it became an inside joke how the longer he was on the prayer walk, the deeper in trouble you would be. One lap around the neighborhood, and things weren't that bad. But don't let him take multiples! It usually was a sign that he really needed to cool off.

But this time was different and a bit confusing. Dad had already levied his verdict. So what's up with the prayer walk? When he got back his countenance had changed. The irritation had been flushed, and in its place was contrition. "Son," he said, "I'm sorry. God's really been dealing with me and my impatience, and what I did to you was sin. God reminded me of this. Will you forgive me?"

Apologies are the voice of the humble. It takes a humble person to say sorry, to acknowledge and confess the wrong. And it is humility that becomes the lifeline to a healthy, vibrant relationship with our children.

When I've failed my children, I have found the first thing I need to do is to take some time to process and pray—as dad did on one of his many prayer walks. God tends to speak to me in these moments, as well as through my wife. And once I've come to the conclusion it's time to apologize, I first own the wrong. I don't say things like, "I'm sorry you took it that way, or you heard it that way," or, "I'm sorry if you felt hurt." These are not apologies, because they subtly redirect ownership from me to their "misperception." A real apology is a wrong owned.

Secondly, apologies are specific in that they name the offense. *I'm sorry for not keeping my word. I'm sorry for yelling at you. I'm sorry for accusing you of lying when you told the truth.*

Finally, apologies should end with what I call "the big ask," which is, "Will you forgive me?" Here, hero dad is placing himself vulnerably at his children's feet, asking them to extend to him grace and mercy.

Maya Angelou once said, "I've learned that people will forget what you said, people will forget what you did, but people will never forget how you made them feel."[1] As the years rolled on, Dad's apologies became more frequent, but in hindsight I don't remember most of what he said. What lingers decades later is how his apologies made me feel: cherished, valued, grateful, amazed. After forgiving my hero, I would watch him make his exit and I would stand amazed at such flawed perfection. Dad's apologies have impressed me more than his strengths.

Chapter 8

THE N-WORD

My father really does believe in this Jesus stuff, and I'm not just talking about what he says to the Chicago Bears, to some church, or from the stage at a big event. Dad eats his Wheaties and he seems to actually enjoy it.

I wasn't there when it happened, but when news of it reached me in my little dorm room in Pennsylvania, I wanted to come straight home and punch this guy in the face. Had it not been for Dad's little rule about me not having my car at school my freshman year, this is exactly what I would have attempted. I'm sure of it.

As the story goes, my father was cruising down Highway 29, not far from our house.

Now, you should know that our community was mostly white, with us being one of the first African American families to move into our neighborhood. Cracker Barrel had just opened their doors not too far from us. There was also a restaurant called the Green Manor, whose building looked like an old antebellum plantation house. And the high school I attended used to be the all-white school before integration. While Jim Crow had released its grip, our community still bore its fingerprints. I was reminded of this constantly, as I saw big pickup trucks with Confederate flags plastered on them. I once remember catching a ride home from school with a girl who happened to be white, when she suddenly demanded I duck down below the dashboard. Unbeknownst to him, her father was driving toward us, and she was sure that if he saw his daughter in a car with a black man, he'd disown her. It was one of the most humiliating moments of my life.

It's in this milieu that my parents raised us. What's more is my chocolate parents reached out to our white neighbors in an honest gesture of friendship and embrace. Much to our dismay, Mom spent a lot of time at our schools where she was constantly voted in as the president of the PTA. And while we were normally the only kids of color on our sports teams, the white parents were frequently engaging ours. They seemed to genuinely love us, and my parents loved them. I never heard Crawford or Karen Loritts talk disparagingly of white people. They never smiled in their faces only to ridicule them behind their backs. All of that was about to get tested.

So my father is cruising down Highway 29 when a man smacks right into him. The airbag engages, bruising Dad's finger. Moments later, my father emerges from the car, somewhat disoriented, trying to find his bearings. But he doesn't have time. The man who hit him happened to be an older white man who begins yelling at my father and calling him the N-word, over and over and over.

My father is a man of integrity, but Saint Crawford he is not. As the story was relayed to me, Dad said his first impulse was to take his big grey brick of a cell phone and engrave the man's forehead with the numbers. He exercised great restraint as this man came marching toward my father while continuing to spew that mother of all epithets. Having no time to go on a prayer walk, I wonder how Dad was able to show such composure. My blood was boiling as I listened.

Not too long after the police came and their report was written, Dad reached out to a friend—a white friend—to go to lunch. Still shaken, Dad shared with him what had just happened. In tears, Dad exhaled, "No matter how much I accomplish, to some people all I will ever be is just another n———." Tragically true.

"So what are you going to do?" I asked Dad at the end of his tale. "Well, I've already forgiven him. I hear we will see each other in court. Pray I get the chance to share the love of Jesus with him."

Some things in life can be sniffed out only through pain and trauma. If I really wanted to know what you believed about something, I'd just need to watch you suffer. Our youngest son is a Chicago Bulls fan who was born in 2004, more than half a decade after Jordan left the team. That's a fan. And I know my parents believe this whole Jesus thing, and this bit about loving all people, even those who mistreat them, because more than bottling up the anger, and erecting an emotional boundary, Dad moved toward this elderly white man with love. Now if that's not eating your Wheaties, I don't know what is.

It's been said Christians are the fifth gospel, the only Bible many in the world will ever read. Not only is the world watching, but so are our children. And they want to know if we take this Jesus thing seriously. When after driving hundreds of miles on the annual summer vacation, and we pull up at the hotel tired, only to discover they botched our reservation, our children are observing how we respond. And when we sit down the next morning at the local diner for breakfast, only to encounter a server who is rude and forgetful, our children are inwardly asking how seriously do we take our faith. And hours later when the person cuts us off on the freeway and speaks to us in sign language, our children are taking notes. Life's inconveniences provide rich opportunities to display our faith and inspire our children to likewise take this Jesus thing seriously—and when you inevitably mess up, just reread the previous chapter and humbly apologize.

I've spent my life addressing America's historic sin of racism, and imploring people to reach across the divide and to love those who look different from them. I do this because I take this Jesus thing seriously. But I also do it because I saw my father take Jesus seriously. More than what my dad said, I was watching what he did. How he treated those who mistreated him was one of the greatest Master Classes he ever offered.

Racism is a learned behavior bequeathed to ensuing generations. And while I believe we all are born deeply flawed and marked by sin, those flaws often get reinforced by parents who do not model integrity. Dads, one of the ways you can be a tailwind for your children is to walk in integrity, especially with those who mistreat you. Your kids are watching.

Chapter 9

ASSUMPTIONS

A child's life is based on assumptions. My children never wonder whether they'll have a house to come home to or a bed to sleep in. They just assume they do. They don't worry about food in the refrigerator or clothes in their closets. These things are assumed to be provided. And the thought doesn't cross their minds whether Dad and Mom will get divorced. Like the rising of the sun, our children assume a stable marriage. These things are so much a part of their subconscious they forecast them into their future. That's right, ask any of my sons, and they will tell you in some way that marriage is their assumption.

One of the saddest days of a child's life is when their assumptions get rattled. My wife can still remember the moment when divorce came knocking on her door, untangling her from her father forever. Here she is, a young girl waving goodbye to her dad, sister, security, and assumptions. I once had a friend who experienced this "tearing asunder," who quipped that divorce is like going to a funeral that never ends. This tends to happen when we are staring at our assumptions in life's proverbial casket.

When assumptions die, new ones tend to take their place. In America, marriage rates continue to decline.[1] Many people are giving up wholesale on the institution, and this makes sense in some ways. If I went through the pain of watching my assumptions of a stable home and family march out the door, I wouldn't be too quick to get married. Why not just move in with someone else and enjoy the spoils of marriage without its covenant? Cohabitation is humanity's understandable attempt at self-preservation.

But my sons desire marriage for the same reason I desired marriage—our assumptions were not rattled by the great intruder of divorce. But there's more. My parents did not merely coexist with one another, sharing a bed and bills. They actually enjoyed each other. I witnessed how Dad loved Mama, making her laugh, and how Mama looked at her husband with adoration—and somewhere along the way, I coveted what they had and wanted to replicate it.

As you know, my father spent a lot of time on airplanes and at venues many miles and days away from us. What made his grueling schedule palatable were the many times we would accompany him on the road. Dad would pull out his calendar, and months in advance, we would plan some one-on-one time with him. I remember joining him in places like New Jersey, Mississippi, Jamaica, and even Africa, to name just a few. These times were precious, and I viewed them as great adventures. I don't remember our conversations or what he preached about, but there is one receipt I continue to hold on to from these trips.

Of course, I'm talking about a pre-smartphone era. These were the days of scrapbooks, Polaroid pictures, and Kodak moments. Dad and I would land at some airport, get our bags, meet our ride, and moments later pull up at the hotel. And when we walked into the room, the first thing Dad would do is to pull out a five-by-seven photo of our family, placing it in some prominent area. Many times this photo would be on the mirror. In my naiveté, I assumed he did this for sentimental reasons because he missed our family. But years later, I would discover there was a greater reason.

I once read *The Autobiography of Malcolm X*, and came to the part where his moral assumptions of his leader, Elijah Muhammad, disintegrated at the revelation of his infidelities. Malcolm remarked how he would have taken a bullet for this man he revered, and never thought such a thing was possible. In the purest sense of the word, Malcolm said he *adored* The Honorable Elijah Muhammad. This is how many children view their fathers. And I too would be devastated if I ever heard of my dad cheating on my mother. The very idea of this is so foreign to me that, had you asked me why Dad put the picture of his wife and children up in the hotel room, I would never have been able to guess the correct answer.

My assumption about my father's moral fortitude ran so deep that I never even thought to ask Dad the question, even as an adult, regarding the picture. The revelation came to me only when I sat in on a session my mother was teaching on marriage. I had long moved out of the house and was pastoring by this time. So when my mother told this audience of men and women that my dad took the picture with him on trips and placed it in prominent places in his hotel rooms because he needed to be reminded there were several people counting on him, and that he shouldn't do anything stupid, I was dumbfounded. But my shock quickly turned to understanding: *Now I get it. That makes total sense.*

My childhood assumptions were never shattered because Dad never assumed integrity. Dad approached his integrity with the same nervous twitch that he had as he parented his oldest son. My father understood that moral integrity is almost like virginity—once you lose it, especially due to sexual reasons, it's hard to get it back. So he went to great lengths—pictures-of-his-family in-hotel-room lengths—to keep his integrity intact.

Great character does not simply happen. It must be planned and fought for. Proverbs 25 likens a man without integrity to a city without walls. Just as builders of ancient cities took great care in constructing the walls because they knew it was the primary defense mechanism of the city, so we dads must likewise put great care into protecting our character. One of the areas in which men must be especially watchful is in the area of sex.

I'm a middle-aged man who experiences temptation, so please do not hear my words as one who has arrived. Instead receive them from a fellow traveler with you on the journey to holiness and sexual fidelity to my bride. I have found it helpful in moments of weakness to press fast-forward and play this thing out. What happens if I have the affair? Proverbs 7 is helpful in getting our arms around the importance of character and integrity when it comes to sex. It tells of a man who is seduced by a married woman, who in the end gives in, and it "cost[s] him his life" (v. 23).

The picture that Proverbs 7 is painting of sin is that it always costs more than it pleases. And yet it is here that the Proverbs 7 father does something masterful by showing his sons the devastating costs that override the fleeting pleasure. At the end, the dad plays the fast-forward game when he writes,

> And now, O sons, listen to me,
>> and be attentive to the words of my mouth.
> Let not your heart turn aside to her ways;
>> do not stray into her paths,
> for many a victim has she laid low,
>> and all her slain are a mighty throng.
> Her house is the way to Sheol,
>> going down to the chambers of death. (vv. 24–27)

In pleading with his sons to be men of integrity, he effectively says, "It's not worth it."

In all my years of pastoring, I've never met a happy adulterer. I have encountered many dads filled with regret over the one-night stand or the affair they thought they could keep secret. The effects have devastated their family, finances, and character. In the end, they agree with the dad in Proverbs 7: it's just not worth it.

Integrity is the best sleep aid on the market. Being fake is a full-time job. The thought of managing a secret life, remembering the right names, how to pay with things so you don't get caught, and covering your tracks is exhausting. But this whole bit about integrity being the best sleep aid is not just for the adults, the dads—it's also for our children. Our kids are at peace when their assumptions about their dads remain in place. Integrity gives our children rest and security in the present, and hope for the possibility of their own marriages for the future.

Chapter 10

GOING FOR BEDROCK

Integrity cannot be white knuckled, as if we wake up every day willing ourselves into exemplary bedrocks of morality. The kinds of people who assume this tend to be the annoying hypocrites who love critiquing how degraded our culture has become while longing for the good old days when prayer sat next to Jim Crow in many of our schools. The men and women I would esteem as models of integrity have the uncanny distinction of never really trying to be, well, people of integrity. Their sights were set on a much loftier goal and along the way they contracted the side effect of integrity.

My wife and I were walking to dinner in downtown San Francisco when we came upon a very well-known building. Not long after being constructed, one of its tenants realized that if they stood on one side of the room and set a ball down, it would slowly roll downhill to the other side. The building is leaning.

When I came across this news, I reached out to a real-estate developer friend of mine who has given oversight to many projects in San Francisco. After some small talk where I made sure to discern in the most clandestine of ways that this architectural faux pas was not of his doing, I asked him about this building. "Oh yes," he chuckled, and then he went on to tell me how much of that part of the city of San Francisco sits on very unstable ground. "Any builder will tell you," he continued, "that to build in this part of the city means you have to go a lot deeper to get to the bedrock. They didn't do that." And without the sure foundation, the building was doomed to lean.

My father never came across as if his real goal in life was to be a "straight building," you know, a person of moral uprightness. All his energy and efforts were placed into going deep and cultivating a vibrant relationship with his God. All integrity necessitates some sort of bedrock. It's never good enough to say you don't want to cheat on your wife, or you don't want to abandon your family or get funny with the money. If there's one thing we learned from the great Prohibition experiment, it is that the fixation on prohibitions causes us to be preoccupied with said prohibitions. Think long enough about not doing something and don't be surprised if you do it. Our attention should be on getting to bedrock.

Examples and discipline are two essentials to nurturing integrity in our lives. Remember, Paul commended Timothy for following "my example" (2 Tim. 3:10). Like an artist at work painting a portrait, we all are in need of someone to look at whose moral beauty is worth mimicking.

This is where the pandemic of fatherlessness becomes so devastating. When men don't see portrait-worthy models of integrity, they are left with a real deficit in fathering their own children. Some years ago, a young man called me in a panic, saying he needed to see me right away. The urgency in his voice compelled me to make room in my calendar, and moments later he barged into my office, collapsed on the sofa, and burst into tears. In the middle of his sobs, he confessed his helplessness as a new father. His dad was never around, and all of the men in his family were leaving legacies of fatherlessness themselves. He needed help, and so we began spending time together, and I was able to encourage him over the years.

You may feel overwhelmed like my friend. The weight of responsibility that's bearing down on you can leave you breathless at times. But I want to encourage you to ask for help. Chances are, if you look carefully around your church, at other fathers or grandfathers whose children play on your kids' teams, or in other places, you will find someone worthy of mimicking. We all need great examples.

But there's more: we need discipline. In an earlier letter to Timothy, Paul encourages him to "train yourself for godliness" (1 Tim. 4:7). Paul is writing in Greek, and it's from the Greek word for "training" that we get the English word *gymnasium*. The word implies sweat, exertion, and hard work. Godliness is consistent character that is consistent with the character of God. Or put another way, godliness is integrity. Notice that Paul says we need to sweat and work hard for it.

I'm guessing at some point in your life you worked out at a gym. You used the cardio machines and lifted the weights. Do this consistently with a healthy eating plan and you'll see results. The same applies when it comes to godly character, except the Bible is our cardio, and prayer along with other disciplines like fasting, silence, and solitude become our weights. Do this enough over an extended period of time and you'll bump into integrity along the way.

In 1964, at a little Church of God in Plainfield, New Jersey, Dad became a Christian. He was just fourteen years old at the time, and this is when he began to take this Jesus thing seriously. Dad, or "CW" as he was known at the time, made a commitment in those early moments of his faith. He decided Jesus would not be some institution or event he attended weekly, but would be a living reality, an active relationship partner in his life. More than anything else, Jesus would get his attention, affections, and pursuit. So, he decided that every day of his life before he would speak to anyone, he would speak to God. And while my father wouldn't say it this way, this daily habit was akin to him going for bedrock—and along the way he ran into integrity.

I cannot tell you how many times I, as a child, walked in on him pouring his heart out to God as if he were pleading with a friend. I still see him now on his knees, face hovering over an open Bible on the edge of his bed. I feel him grabbing my arm on one of those road trips there in our hotel room with Mom and my siblings looking out at us from their place on the mirror, beckoning me to seek God's blessings with him as he was about to preach to a waiting audience. I can see the joy in his face as he relayed to us his encounter with God during his monthly day away for fasting and prayer at some retreat center. And I still see his horrible handwriting in one of his prayer journals. All of these exercises were Dad grabbing the "drill," and going for bedrock.

Integrity is a lot like humility in that you don't advertise that's who you are or what you've become. It's more like a beautiful person walking into a room. No need to announce that's who you are, or try to impress. Just go about your business and watch people steal glimpses.

There's an ancient proverb that pretty much says a good name is to be desired above riches (Prov. 22:1). I'm thankful my father has left me a good name, because anyone with the last name Loritts is directly related to us. I can't tell you how many times people have heard my peculiar name and veered off into some story about my father. And while on my more ornery days I have to catch my eyes from rolling like that ball gathering steam on its way to the other side of the room in that bedrockless San Francisco building, some of their stories make me proud. I've heard tales of my father being invited to speak at some gathering and refusing an honorarium, choosing instead to reallocate those dollars to help get the new fledgling organization he spoke for on their feet. Or the time my father stayed up all night pleading with a man not to divorce his wife. Or the time when a woman got on an elevator with him in one of those faraway hotels, followed him to his floor, and then tried to go to his room when my dad sprayed some female repellent on her by confessing his love and affection for his God, wife, and children.

And yes, I've stolen glimpses of my dad's moral beauty, collecting a treasure trove of character stories of my own. But it never appears as if my father is really trying hard to be a person of integrity. I'm sure being a man of integrity was difficult at times, and he's had his share of close calls. But these decisions seem more reflexes than exertions. This tends to happen when for fifty years you've been drilling down into bedrock.

More than leaving our children a monetary inheritance, we need to leave them a greater legacy of a good name (see Prov. 22:1). But the focus cannot be on having a good name. If that is our focus, then we will become the CEOs of our own PR management firm. Our reputations are who people think we are, but our character is who we actually are. Obsess over the former at the expense of the latter, and you're a hypocrite in the making. But take care of character, and the reputation will take care of itself. We take care of character by going for bedrock. When God becomes our goal, when drilling for bedrock becomes our aim, we will catch integrity along the way. May our foundations go deep into the God who created us, loves us, and calls us into a vibrant relationship with Himself.

PART 3

TEACHING

Great dads gift their children with a kind of
upright teaching that prepares them to meet the
challenges of life and walk in their God-ordained
purpose. Doing this well necessitates vision and
intentionality.

Chapter 11

THE TENURED
PROFESSOR

Fathers are the tenured professors of their homes. Our children will graduate with a degree either in manhood or what to expect from a man with just about all of the classes taught by Dr. Dad. They are watching our work ethic, how we relate to women, how we handle money, how we deal with conflict, and a whole host of other things we do. When our kids graduate from our homes, they will either copy and paste the lessons learned from us or make up their minds to go in the opposite direction. I have friends who refuse to touch alcohol because of what it did to their father. I also know of men who treat women in a condescending way, a way they learned from their father. To be a dad is to be in a perpetual state of teaching.

Paul recognized the importance of teaching. Writing to his son in the faith, Timothy, he explained, "All Scripture is breathed out by God and profitable for *teaching*, for reproof, for correction, and for training in righteousness, that the man of God may be complete, equipped for every good work" (2 Tim. 3:16–17, emphasis mine). Paul was an ethnic Jew whose worldview had been shaped by a book the Jews referred to as the Torah, or the Law. One of the most famous sections of the Law is found in Deuteronomy 6, a text the ancient Jews referred to as the *Shema*. The Jews prayed this ancient text many times a day. But what cannot be lost in the repetition is the importance of fathers, the home, and teaching:

> Hear, O Israel: The LORD our God, the LORD is one. You shall love the LORD your God with all your heart and with all your soul and with all your might. And these words that I command you today shall be on your heart. You shall teach them diligently to your children, and shall talk of them when you sit in your house, and when you walk by the way, and when you lie down, and when you rise. You shall bind them as a sign on your hand, and they shall be as frontlets between your eyes. You shall write them on the doorposts of your house and on your gates. (Deut. 6:4–9)

While Deuteronomy does not explicitly mention that fathers do the teaching, the gender ambiguity assumes the father is at least participating alongside his wife in the development of his children by teaching them the ways of God. Psalm 78 makes it even clearer that fathers are to teach their children. The psalmist writes,

> He established a testimony in Jacob
>   and appointed a law in Israel,
> which he commanded our fathers
>   to teach to their children,
> that the next generation might know them,
>   the children yet unborn,
> and arise and tell them to their children,
>   so that they should set their hope in God
> and not forget the works of God,
>   but keep his commandments. (Ps. 78:5–7)

As Israel was on the precipice of finally ending her sojourn in the wilderness and poised to enter the Promised Land, God was concerned the secular nations around her would be an enticing gravitational force pulling her away from Him. But beyond this, God wanted to see Israel be a vehicle of blessing, where the ways of God would infiltrate these idolatrous nations. So how was God going to accomplish this? Notice God's means were not going to come through elected officials or large synagogue gatherings, but via the home. The home was to be God's domestic church where Pastor Dad became the curator of the words and promises of God. Dad was to always teach of the faithfulness of God to his children, who in turn would go out, establish their own homes, and teach their children. Dads teaching children was to be the impetus for healthy homes and a transformed world.

If you were to visit the home I grew up in, say around six in the evening, you would see a long picnic table in the middle of our kitchen, with a yellow phone fixed into the wall with a long yellow cord dangling from it. Around the table would be plates and glasses—normally jars filled with water or juice. At the head of the table would be Dad, whose Bible was stationed prominently above his plate. Mom would be next to him, and my baby sister, Holly, was in her high chair. Heather and Bryndan, my other siblings, were also seated. Many times there was an extra plate out for one of our friends from school we had invited over. You could see the awkwardness in their faces as we would grab hands and listen as Dad would pray the blessing.

Soon after, eating and laughter would merge as we shared about our day. Then, when Dad sensed we were finishing, he would open up the Scriptures and read a chapter, offering commentary along the way. Again, you'll have to forgive me if I forget the intricacies of his lessons. While I'm sure some things stuck, the image of him showing up and reading the Bible stands much taller in my mind. And the sight of a black man sitting next to his black wife of several decades, reading the Bible, became too much for my friends like Deontaye and Deomni to handle (actual names of friends, by the way). They simply had no paradigm or category to file the image. And while no ethnicity holds a monopoly on the pandemic of fatherlessness, it is especially viral in the black community. Overwhelmed by the visual, my friends would usually confide that in some way these dinners gave them hope as they looked at my fatherhood poster.

Recently, my father made the long trek across country to visit our family. All of us, especially our boys, were so excited to see him. We made a feast, set the table, and heard those familiar sounds of eating and laughter merge as we enjoyed each other's company. And as my father had done years ago, when I sensed the meal was coming to a close, I grabbed my Bible, opened it, and read a chapter from the Scriptures, offering commentary along the way. I also asked some questions, mainly of my children. And as they began to share, I stole a glimpse of the old man who seemed as if he was about to be overcome with emotion. I'm not sure why he was so moved. We've never spoken about that evening at my home. But if I had to guess, his mind had wandered back a few decades and thousands of miles, where at a picnic table with a yellow phone and a Bible it all began. Life was coming full circle. What he had taught was being replicated.

You may feel somewhat intimidated by the notion of leading your family through the teaching of God's Word. Maybe you think a seminary degree or mastery of the Bible's original languages are a prerequisite. That's not true. The ancient Greeks, experts in the art of rhetoric, observed how one of the marks of transformative communicators is what they called *ethos*, from which we get the word *ethics*. The Greeks said the speakers who moved you the most were those who weren't just talking from their heads but from the overflow of their lives. This encourages me as a dad. You don't need to spend a second in Bible college or know a shred of Hebrew. All you need is a life committed to Jesus, and to speak from the overflow of that life to your children.

Chapter 12

BEDROOM HOMILIES

My father spanked us. I don't know how that makes you feel, and please don't think that what you are about to read is going to be some treatise on how the demise of our country is due to kids not being spanked enough or at all. While I have never understood the rationale of the parent who barters with her three-year-old that if she would just sit still long enough so mommy can finish her conversation, she'll pick her up some chicken strips and French fries for dinner, I do get that we all parent differently.

We didn't have a time-out ministry in our house. There was no counting to three, parental pleading for us to obey, or going back and forth. In the Loritts home, you got one time to get it right, and if you didn't there were consequences.

THE DAD DIFFERENCE

It's important for you to understand that we feared Mama. As you know, Mama was from the inner city of Philadelphia, where she used to live on some street called "Diamond." It sounds elegant, I know. But if you ever go to Philadelphia, I would seriously caution you against going to any street named "Diamond" or "Martin Luther King." Yes, I know he stood for peace and integration, but most streets across the country bearing his name are anything but peaceful or integrated. Mama's posture on behavior was simple: if you wanted to act a fool, she'll act one with you, right where you are, anywhere, any time. We got it in grocery stores, bathrooms, restaurants, churches, cars, schools, the home, the front yard, the backyard, at friends' homes ("Excuse me, dinner was so lovely. Where's your bathroom? I need to have a moment with Bryan."), and I'm sure several more places. Mama was not abusive, but—boy—she didn't play.

Mama was law, Dad was grace. On more than one occasion, he would return from one of those prayer walks and say something about how he had angered God many times in his life, and God gave him grace, so it was only right if he gave us grace in return. This response became so frequent that we learned not to look excited, quickly utter thanks, and go outside. I can see Mama shaking her head slowly, where I'm pretty sure she was thinking her man had gone soft.

But there were also plenty of moments when Dad came home from the prayer walk and would gently instruct us to go to his room. We knew what that meant.

Most of the spankings I received had to do with me cutting up in church. I've written in some of my other books about how the church I grew up in didn't have any air-conditioning. When you couple this with it being in Atlanta, Georgia, in the middle of summer and it's a black church, which meant at least three hours in service where we had to put on a suit and snap on one of those ties while the usher passed out little wooden sticks with cardboard stapled onto them, where one side was a picture of Dr. Martin Luther King and the other side an advertisement for a funeral home, you can see how it was hard for me to pay attention and not cut up while Sister Johnson caught the Holy Ghost.

As it goes, this one day my father was sitting on the pulpit where he had been invited by our pastor to preach. The choir was finishing up their "B" selection, which is the last of two songs they sing in the traditional African American church right before the pastor is to preach, when I found myself on the back row cutting up with my friend Dante. In the middle of my shenanigans, Dad caught my eye and motioned with his index finger for me to join him onstage. Somewhat in disbelief, I pointed to myself and then turned around to make sure he wasn't motioning to someone behind me. Dad gave one of those "I'm so annoyed with you" smiles and motioned again for me to come onstage. Rising from my seat, I took the long walk of shame down the center aisle while Sister Fussell was singing her heart out in the choir. I could feel the eyes of about five hundred people on my back. When I finally reached the stage, Dad laid his hand on my shoulder and whispered in my ear something along the lines of what I could expect when the message ended and we returned home. Then he told me to return to my seat. As I passed my mother in the front row, I could have sworn I saw her smile and clinch her fist at Dad the way a person does when their teammate just made a great shot. I'm sure she was thinking Dad was not being soft anymore.

Dad preached his heart out, and then we made the long journey home. There was no prayer walk this time. He calmly instructed for me to go to his room where by now I knew the routine. I'll spare you all but one of the details. Whenever Dad spanked us, he would always first sit down and open up the Bible and read a chapter from the book of Proverbs, where he would go on about the difference between the wise person and the fool. He would say something like how the whole book of Proverbs can be summed up with the word *listen*. Fools don't listen, while wise people do. And then he would always end by saying that what we had done had hurt the heart of God who created us and loves us and wants us to experience life to the full. And as I write, I'm pretty proud of myself for remembering all this, because I do recall thinking, "Just get it over with."

Life's greatest lessons often lie in the residuals. Sure, Dad's bedroom homilies were important in correcting my behavior, but as an adult with three children of my own, Dad's way of disciplining me has informed the way I have disciplined my children. And when I speak of "the way," I'm not talking about the specific method of spanking. Dad's bedroom homilies have given me the "ABCs" of how to discipline my children.

The first thing we fathers should do is to address our anger. Anger in itself is not sinful. If it were, God the Father and Jesus would be sinful. Bible scholars point out that one of the character traits of God is anger or wrath, and we see Jesus filled with righteous anger when He sees the temple being misused by people for their own greed. Anger is actually a sign of love. This is why the Bible says that, prior to coming to Christ, we were "by nature children of wrath" (Eph. 2:3). You may wonder how God can simultaneously love us and be angry with us. Well, anyone with children understands that anger and love can coexist, because nobody can quite tick us off like the ones we love. So when our children do foolish things and anger us, it's actually a good thing, because it shows we care. Be concerned if you are indifferent.

So in those moments when our children act, well, like children and do foolish things, the first thing we should do is *address our anger* by taking time to cool off. Maybe go on a prayer walk where you not only talk to God but also allow your emotions to settle. Set a time to come back and revisit the offense. You never want to discipline in a state of emotional anger. I think this is one reason why Paul said, "In your anger do not sin" (Eph. 4:26 NIV).

Second, we should *be in control*. When Korie's and my children were younger, there were times when we spanked them. The book of Proverbs talks about spanking: "Folly is bound up in the heart of the child, but the rod of discipline drives it far from him" (Prov. 22:15). Many parents don't agree with spanking, and that's fine. I in no way want to argue over a method of discipline. The point is that however we choose to discipline, we should be in control of our emotions. So when our children did something particularly foolish, I would always announce to them how many points of contact they could expect. In fact, over time they would beat me to it by asking, "How many, Daddy?" By announcing a number (usually three or five), I was communicating that Daddy's in control and is not disciplining them out of unrighteous anger.

Finally, be sure to remember the aim is to *correct* and not to punish. Discipline should have an aim and never be punitive. This is the message of Hebrews 12:3–9, where the writer positions God as our Father, and we as his sons and daughters. It is out of our Father's love for us that He disciplines us, the writer says. His aim is that we become holy (Heb. 12:14), which is to be like Him. It's good, then, to ask yourself, *What am I trying to accomplish when I discipline my child?* Ask this question before you discipline, because the answer will in many ways feed the kind of discipline you choose to use. For example, there will be times when taking away the television or certain privileges will prove way more effective in accomplishing your aim than spanking. And it's also good to consider how our children are naturally wired, and tailor the discipline accordingly. Sending my introverted middle son to his room for the night was like sending Br'er Rabbit to the brier patch—much more a reward than correction. But sending my extroverted youngest to his room would be like forcing me to eat Wheaties.

In hindsight, Dad's homilies helped to put my foolish behavior in its proper place. Dad was not disciplining me because he was angry with me. Discipline was never personal with him. His bedroom homilies were his attempt to stitch my behavior to the heart of God. He was more hurt that I had hurt God than him. To Dad, if the bottom line of discipline was creating compliant children who obeyed only because that's what their parents wanted, it would miss the point altogether. These kinds of kids may make wonderful twelve-year-olds, but usually they go crazy once they leave home. Their "obedience" flew at too low of an altitude.

There must be a greater moral compass than parental compliance. For Dad, it was the fear of God.

But I learned something else from Dad's bedroom homilies. Because Dad connected my behavior to God, it was hard for me to hold a grudge with my father. "It's not about me," was the message Dad was sending. Or as Sonny said to Michael in *The Godfather,* "This ain't personal." I needed to know this. Children need to know this.

PART 4

EXPERIENCES

Great fathers place a premium on giving their children the RITE kind of experiences over gifts. Things wear out and expire. Experiences endure, marking us forever.

Chapter 13

THE AIRPLANE

Some years ago, I was on an airplane. When about seven or eight thousand feet in the air, climbing to our cruising altitude, we heard a loud boom and then saw a trail of smoke sprinting from the left engine. I quickly surveyed the flight attendants, and the look on their faces was one of deep concern if not outright panic. An eerie silence fell on the cabin. Seconds later, I heard the right engine race, and not long after, we were circling back to our airport of origin where minutes later we were on solid ground. Pheeew!

About a week later, I talked to some pilots who were part of our church and told them what happened. I asked them why the pilot decided to race the right engine. Without thinking, they said that had the pilot not done so, we may have flipped over in the air and plummeted to our deaths. "How long did the pilot have to make that decision?" I asked. "Oh, a few seconds." But I shouldn't worry, they continued. Their hours of training had ingrained into them this reflex reaction. Experience had saved the day.

When I board a plane, I don't wonder about the pilot's educational pedigree or how smart they are. I want to know how many hours they have flying under their belts. And when I'm on the operating table drifting off with my body entrusted into the hands of a doctor, I don't want this surgery to be his first. I want him to be experienced.

Experience matters. All experiences shape us—good ones and bad ones. When Dad would get agitated with us because of some poor decision we made, he would often quip, "Experience isn't always the best teacher, but it is the only school the fool will attend." In context, he was saying that some people will learn only the hard way, through negative experiences. In the Bible, the book of Proverbs alludes to this when the writer says that "the way of transgressors is hard" (Prov. 13:15 KJV).

When we took our children on their first cruise, my youngest son asked me for money to buy an ice cream cone. I shook my head, telling him he didn't need any money. "Wait a minute," he said, "you mean to tell me I can just go and get another cone without giving them any money?" I nodded my head in the affirmative. You could see the wheels turning in his ten-year-old mind. "So you're telling me, I can get as many ice cream cones as I want without having to pay any money?" Again, I nodded my head and then added, "But I don't think it's a good idea to eat too much ice cream, because you'll get sick." After his third ice cream cone in about thirty minutes, Korie was pleading with me to stop him. I never did. Over half a dozen ice cream cones later, he was sprawled out on the bed complaining of a tummy ache. Ever since then, I've never had to warn him about the perils of eating too much ice cream.

We've all been there, haven't we? We know what it's like to sit in the classroom of bad decisions and unfortunate experiences. You may be meticulous about paying off the credit card in full every month because you spent years in credit card debt with seemingly no way out. Or you may be really diligent in saving because there was that time when life came at you fast, and you were stuck out in the rain without a rainy-day fund. Bad experiences have a way of marking us, don't they?

But this section is not about giving your kids *bad* experiences but about the power of providing the right (or *RITE*) kind of experiences. Every father will give his children experiences, but the question is whether he is giving them the right kind of experiences.

When Phil Jackson was the head coach of the Los Angeles Lakers, one of his biggest challenges was getting his star center Shaquille O'Neal to shoot better from the free throw line. Shaq would spend hours shooting free throws. One day after practice, a reporter noticed all of the hard work and effort he was putting in, but there just didn't seem to be any results. So the reporter quoted the well-known sentiment about how practice is supposed to make perfect. Phil Jackson shook his head and replied, "Practice doesn't make perfect, it makes permanent." So what if you spend a lot of time working on something if you're doing it the wrong way. Progress is made in doing it the right way.

We've been talking some about a father-son relationship in the Bible between Paul and his spiritual son, Timothy. The two formed an impenetrable bond as they logged hundreds if not thousands of hours going from city to city in the Roman Empire. Paul's life inspired Timothy, and moments from death, Paul seizes the opportunity to deliver to Timothy yet another letter filled with teaching. But there's more. Along the way, Paul provided Timothy with enriching experiences, the right kind of experiences, which played a significant role into shaping him into the kind of person he was. Timothy accompanied Paul on his various journeys, occupying a front-row seat as he watched how Paul conducted himself as a man and minister. Later, Paul would send Timothy in his stead to instruct the church at Corinth in the ways of Christ (1 Cor. 4:17). And anxious to hear about how the church at Philippi was doing but unable to get there because of his incarceration for the gospel, Paul sent Timothy to get a report (Phil. 2:19). This became a key part of young Timothy's job—representing his father in the faith to various churches and bringing back a report (see 1 Thess. 3:1–2). Ultimately, these experiences would become vital as he would take his post as the pastor at the church of Ephesus, drawing on his wealth of good experiences to faithfully lead the people of God.

Paul's use of hands-on experiences to raise his children in the ministry became a core curriculum in his handbook of spiritual fathering. Jesus did the same with His disciples when He sent them out in Matthew 10. Again, Malcolm Gladwell had it right when he argued that greatness is not so much a matter of natural talent, or even consuming mountains of information, but hard, repetitious work done right—what he calls the ten-thousand-hour rule,[1] or what we may call the *RITE* experiences. What's true for would-be pastors and hall-of-fame musicians and athletes must also be true of great dads who set up their children for success. Tailwind dads give their kids rich, positive experiences.

Chapter 14

THE BAT

Walking into my friend's home, one of the first things you notice is a bat mounted on a wall with two words carved into it: *RESPECT HER*. Littered around these words are a collection of signatures. Talk about peculiar. It was my first visit to his home, and he was trying to give me the obligatory tour, but I wasn't having it this day. I just had to get some intel from him about the bat.

You should know this friend is so much more than a friend. We're not even peers really. Like Paul with Timothy, he's a father to me even though we don't share DNA. When I'm weighted down with a major decision, there's no such thing as me pulling the trigger without calling him. And for sure, when I'm in one of those seasons when I'm feeling more like a headwind than a tailwind to my wife and children, I call this man who has released six phenomenal "arrows" from his home, and has loved his wife for about half a century now. So he needed to give up the goods on the bat.

My friend poured a few glasses of iced tea, and we sat down in the living room with the bat peering over us. "Well, as you know, I have six children with four of those being daughters, and when they started dating in high school, there was no such thing as some strange man coming over to my home to take them out without me first getting to know them." *This story's going to be good*, I thought as I inched forward in my seat. He went on to explain how if a guy expressed a desire to take one of his daughters out, he had to come over before the anticipated date for a little one-on-one interview with him. Seated together on the deck, my friend brought out several files containing financial records like bank statements. He then encouraged the would-be suitor to look at the documents, and without fail the young man would turn him down. How could a complete stranger spend time with something so personal, so valuable? Then, smiling, my friend pointed out the irony of how they were asking for access to someone even more valuable to him than those bank statements—his daughter. You could see the lights starting to come on. Then moving in for the climax, my mentor asked some more questions, and if he was satisfied, he would let him know what was permissible on the date—you know what they weren't going to do with their hands and lips (not to mention a few parts of their anatomy), how long they were going to be out, and so on. If the young man agreed, there was one more thing that had to be done before he was green-lighted. The bat was brought out. (For some reason, I envisioned one of his sons, donned in a tuxedo with tails and white gloves, carrying the bat on a silver platter. But I'm sure that's not how it went down.) The two words noticed, and a signature rendered. Finally, his daughter could breathe a sigh of relief. They were going out.

Now, I know some can take this story the wrong way, misinterpreting my friend as being a bully or creating some narrative of women being completely helpless and clueless, in need of a man's salvation, like a throwback to some bygone era—which wasn't true, then or now. But this would miss the point and my friend's heart by more than a mile. This father was trying to take his role as protector seriously. And even more so, he wanted to model to his daughters how men are to treat women as being valuable.

As my friend regaled me with this story, one of his daughters came into the room. It had been more than a decade since she had experienced these interviews, and by now she was on her way to being married. I wanted to know how she felt. She admitted on one hand to a touch of embarrassment, but she chalked that up to being in high school and the ever-present longing for approval. In hindsight, she commented, she was grateful for these experiences of watching her father step up to protect her; it gave her a much-needed blueprint for what to look for in a husband.

Sociologists will look back on the early part of the twenty-first century and remark how this was the era of #METOO where powerful men were finally called on the carpet for exploiting women in order to satisfy their carnal appetites. Like all of the video-documented instances of racism, the narrative of men using their power to exploit is not new, just finally exposed for the world to see.

Most Jewish women who were prostitutes in antiquity had at one point been married.[1] Due to widowhood or husbands who no longer wanted to be with them, they were forced into the only occupation where they could provide for themselves. To be an unmarried woman in antiquity was the epitome of vulnerability, leaving one totally susceptible to the whims of men.

All this makes the case of Ruth and Boaz peculiar. If ever there was a person who was poised to be abused on life's proverbial casting couch, it was Ruth. Her husband had died, leaving her childless. She was an immigrant and poor, on the brink of starvation. It's also safe to say she was easy on the eyes, as my grandmother often quipped. We know this because her first day on the job, boss-man Boaz notices her and asks, "Whose young woman is this?" (Ruth 2:5). When he discovers she's an immigrant and vulnerable, he gives orders to his men to protect her (2:9). Talk about countercultural. It would have been nothing for him as both the man and the overseer of her work environment to have his way with her.

This now brings us to chapter three in the story of Ruth, one of the most controversial scenes in the Bible. When Naomi pieces together Ruth's initial encounter with Boaz, and how Boaz is their kinsman redeemer, she instructs Ruth to go to the threshing floor at night where Boaz would likely be feeling the effects of his drinking wine (3:7), and tells her to lay at his feet. What does all of this mean?

Conservative scholar Daniel Block writes how the threshing

floor at harvest time was often seen as "a place of illicit sexual behavior."[2] Robert L. Hubbard observes in the New International Commentary on the Old Testament that Naomi's "words are tantalizingly ambiguous and replete with suggestive sexual innuendo."[3] And cultural scholar Tamara C. Eskenazi says, "But in the ancient world, to speak of a woman uncovering any part of a man's body at night was highly suggestive" (see the JPS commentary notes on this verse).

However confusing Ruth's actions were on this evening, we can still conclude in the scheme of things that she is a virtuous woman, just as Boaz is described as being a virtuous man (Ruth 2:1), in spite of his wine-induced intoxication. Aren't you glad that one moment, even one misinterpreted moment, doesn't define the totality of who we are?

But let us not forget Ruth is not only a Moabite, unfamiliar with the cultural practices of the people of God, but she is also a woman who is materially and sociologically insecure, with no man to cover her. There is no husband. There is no son. A part of the challenge is her worldview had been shaped by a culture that said a woman's worth is found only in being married and having children. She has neither, and the result is a devastating insecurity that propelled her to make an aggressively, confusing leap toward a man.

While we are in need of more virtuous women like Ruth, there does seem to be a growing trend of insecure young ladies who are acting out in sexually aggressive ways. Please don't hear me as saying women should be docile and passive, lacking any kind of ambition when it comes to their careers. If you think this is what I'm saying, let's schedule a time for you and my bride to have coffee. Let me say it in my Yoda voice: "Docile, Korie Loritts is not." Women should have goals and ambitions and a deep drive toward accomplishment, whether it's outside the home and in the marketplace, at home, or both. But what I'm cautioning against is women pursuing men to satisfy their sexual proclivities. And, yes, while men bear the brunt of the blame for our sexual aggression and the ways it has brought severe historical harm to women, I'm interested in this chapter not so much in this behavior in women, but why they are often driven in this direction and our culpability as dads.

I talk to young men frequently about their struggles to walk the path of purity. It's more than enough to deal with the internal fire of sexual desire. But they also comment on how they sometimes get propositioned by girls for oral sex and intercourse. I'd like to believe I was a good-looking brotha in high school, but this never happened to me. Sure, there was the rare whisperings of the aggressive woman (she's been around since Proverbs 7), but this was more of an aberration, whereas today it's become quite the norm. What's changed?

When a father puts down his bat, abdicating his responsibility to protect, we leave our daughters not only vulnerable but thirsty for intimacy. Insecurity now moves in, creating in some women irresponsible patterns of relating to men. Young women on the hunt aren't climbing in the bed so much for sex as they are looking for Boaz, and Boaz should have been in the delivery room when they came into the world, at their recitals when they were little girls, being faithful to their mamas on the business trip, and out on the deck with bat in hand protecting and collecting signatures as they were readying for their first date.

Some years ago, during an interview with Oprah, the comedian Chris Rock was basking in the birth of his daughter. When asked about his hopes for her, Chris famously responded, "I'm just trying to keep her off the pole." While his words elicited laughs from the audience, his vision for his daughter was neither lofty nor compelling. Tragically, this "vision" for our daughters is shared by way too many fathers.

With the recent renouncement of his faith, Joshua Harris— the author of the famous *I Kissed Dating Goodbye* and a de facto architect of the Christian purity movement—has caused the Christian community to reflect on the purity culture, which rose to popularity during the turn of the twentieth century. I remember sitting in youth groups where I heard everything about the evils of fornication. I watched as friends of mine received promise rings from their parents, vowing to go to their wedding beds as virgins. I even remember a well-known pastor sending his daughter to the doctor before her marriage to ensure she was still a virgin, then having a certificate printed verifying her virginity and posting it online. Along the way, I felt an eerie unease. Is this what being a Christian is all about, just refraining from sexual immorality? Should the loftiest vision a father has for his daughters be to "keep them off the pole"?

I think you know the answer. Paul often exhorts his followers to *put off* certain things and to *put on* certain things (Col. 3:5, 10). To Paul, the Christian life is both a turning away and a turning to. It's not enough to stay away from sex; we must turn to Christ.

Since this is true, then the aim of the Christian life is to treasure Christ. When Christ becomes my everything, this works in us a deep sense of security, where I do not need to turn to idols of sex, acceptance, and worldly love to find validation. Staying "off the pole" then becomes symptomatic of a woman whose affections lie not in her beauty or words of affirmation from others, but in her God. Tailwind dads paint this vision for their daughters.

So what does Boaz do when he wakes up in the middle of the night to discover Ruth is there? We would more than understand if he would have taken advantage of her. Instead, he shocks us by refusing to exploit her, and instead assures Ruth he will do everything to redeem her. Boaz sees past her body and into her heart. He knows there's something far deeper at play.

Again, Boaz is described as a "worthy man" (Ruth 2:1)—a man full of substance and rich with character. He's driven more by principle than impulse. Had Ruth's dad been into the whole bat thing, Boaz's signature would have been the most prominent, the most meaningful. Boaz is anything but a boy; he's a godly man.

Boys exploit. Men protect. Boys are led by their appetites. Men are governed by God-honoring principles. Boys see women as a conglomeration of body parts. Men see women as created in the image of God. Our society is suffering from a deficiency of Boaz men, worthy men who will model for their daughters what to look for in a man, and when they find a man may he be in the ilk of Boaz. Dads, this starts with us. We can rewrite the narrative of deeply insecure women who act out in sexually aggressive ways to fill the void left by a dad who was more boy than he was man. We have plenty of boys. What our daughters need are Boaz men. And no, you may not need to use a baseball bat with the words *RESPECT HER* engraved on it. But may we all step up to the plate as men and speak to the deepest places of our daughters' hearts.

Chapter 15

THE DUMP

One year, as we were saying goodbye to our kids, we made them pose for the obligatory "my parents just dropped us off at camp and are about to post this on Instagram" picture. And to our amazement, as if planned, they broke out into these poses projecting a hardened image as if life had been cruel to them and where smiles were prohibited because they could be perceived as a sign of weakness. Korie and I quickly gave them the "you've got to be kidding me" look, while I went ahead and snapped the picture. Moments later I uploaded the pic to a few of our social media platforms and inserted #StraightOutOfACuldesac.

Our kids have it pretty easy. They've each attended both public and private schools, played on club teams, gone out to eat at some pretty nice restaurants, stayed in great hotels, and vacationed in a lot of cool places. While we are nowhere near wealthy by American standards, we are by global standards, which feels like a strangely foreign admission.

When the biggest questions of one's day-to-day life tend to be, "What outfit will I wear? Where will we eat after church on Sunday? Will my parents let me drive the car across town to hang with my friends?" feelings of entitlement set in. This happens when one consumes while providing little to no contribution. Entitled people suffer from a myopia of sorts where they can't see outside themselves. Life is all about them, and everyone in their sphere is expected to orbit around, well, them.

There are moments as a dad when I catch a whiff of entitlement's stench. Like the time I came home from work one day and my oldest, who was ten at the time, was on the sofa watching his favorite kids' show, with the remote in hand, his legs crossed, a bag of cookies at his side, and nursing a cup of juice. Well, I guess his mother and I were talking too loud, because he paused his program and told us we needed to keep it down. Everything slowed down, and I took in the whole scene. It's one thing to be shushed by your child, but it's another when that child has the television you paid for paused, with cookie crumbs and juice that you purchased dotting the edges of his mouth, and has an attitude while sitting in the comforts of your home that you work hard to provide as you are trying to catch up on the day with the woman who birthed him. I took a deep breath, channeled my father, and ventured outdoors for my first prayer lap around the neighborhood.

I was becoming acutely aware that the gravitational pull to my children's hearts—and all of ours for that matter—was downward into themselves, into entitlement. And if I did nothing, I would release from our home narcissistic arrows who did not hit their transcendent targets, but instead lived for themselves. Something had to change.

A few months after my entitlement-induced prayer walk, my oldest son and I found ourselves on an airplane headed for Honduras to build homes, serve orphans, and feed the destitute. As we climbed out to 35,000 feet, my mind wandered back to the days when my father took me with him on missions trips with the sole purpose of caring for the marginalized and sharing the good news of Jesus Christ. These trips surprised me. I had assumed I was going to help these "poor helpless people," when I was the poor one needing to be rescued by Jesus through the very ones I had come to serve.

Over the next several days, sweat drained off my son's forehead, and I stole glimpses of him massaging the ache in his shoulder brought on by hammering. On breaks, he would play soccer with some of the children from the orphanage. Well, he'd be more a spectator than a player, as he would watch them take the ball from him over and over again. Then, as the sun was setting, we'd gather for prayer and worship, just us dads and our sons, along with the leadership and children from the orphanage. Our time would end with sharing—more the kids from the orphanage sharing and us trying our best to listen to their painful tales. In gentle, kid-sensitive language, our interpreters would relay the tear-filled stories from these kids, most of them having to do with sexual abuse: A kid about the age of my son, whose poverty-stricken parents made him go out and dig graves. The only problem was that the men on his work detail forced him to do awful things to them if he wanted to collect his day's wages. Others talked of being leased to adults in order to provide for their families. Several times I wanted to excuse my son from the room, but he needed to hear these stories. Glancing at him during these moments of painful vulnerability, his eyes were far more transfixed on these children than they had ever been on his favorite Nickelodeon show. I draped my arm over his shoulders.

Our trip ended with us serving at a place the locals refer to simply as "The Dump." True to its name, this is the place where most of the waste in Tegucigalpa ends up. After some instructions in which we were sternly told to stick close to one another lest we be mobbed, we piled into our pickup trucks and made our way out to this city of refuse.

I knew we were getting close because the stench was overpowering. My esophagus tightened, and my son and I quickly reached for our bandanas to cover our nose and mouth. One of the dads pointed to what appeared to be scores of vultures hovering as if in a holding pattern over the mounds of human waste. And then, another dad began to cry as he pointed to a pregnant woman sifting through the garbage looking for her next meal. We must have seen a few hundred people who had become citizens of the dump, their tents and shanties in plain sight claiming their home. We saw children, men, pregnant women, and families. Our car stopped. My son was frozen, but not by fear, it seemed. He was immobilized by a terrible awe, the kind of awe that comes from something you had not just never seen, but could never imagine.

We stood on the back of our pickup trucks, handing out

water and food to the gathering crowd, while one of our leaders preached the good news of Jesus Christ. My son gave water while holding on to my leg like he was dangling from a cliff on the precipice of death. When our supply of food and water was exhausted, we took our seats and began the journey home, as once again the sun was setting. No one said a word.

Soon we packed our things, said our goodbyes, and boarded our plane. And even though we shared a few words, the aftertaste of silence still mingled among our departing group. These few days in Central America were engraved on the walls of my son's memory.

Once back, the change in my son was striking. No one had to tell him to eat all of his food, to clean up after himself, or to make his bed. There was a self-imposed temporary moratorium on shushing his mom and dad while he watched *The Suite Life of Zack & Cody*. Korie begged me to schedule trips for his other two brothers.

Now, of course, the change, while striking, was also fleeting. But in thinking about our experience at the dump and the impact it made on my oldest, two things stand out: exposure and work.

Dads, we are the architects of our kids' normal. If all our kids are exposed to are warm beds, clothing we provide, food they enjoy, extracurricular activities that cost us an arm and a leg, and safe environments where little to nothing is required of them in terms of contribution, then we are raising entitled children. This is their normal. "Of course I need to have the latest iPhone." "Of course I should be on social media." It's really easy to complain about four-year-old soccer leagues where everyone gets a trophy and there are no real winners or losers, but we never ask the question of who created that system. That would be the parents. Dads, we are often guilty of being accomplices to the crime of entitlement.

One of the most helpful things we can do is to take them out of their norm and place them in settings that are both literally and proverbially miles away from what they are used to. For the good of our children's souls, they need to serve in a soup kitchen, stand on a dump passing out water, or build some home for an impoverished family that is nowhere near living "The Suite Life." This demands intentionality on our parts, to give them vital experiences by exposing them to and immersing them in seas of overwhelming poverty and neediness, where the biggest questions aren't how many likes did they get on their latest Instagram post, but where is their next meal coming from? Tailwind dads are intentional in giving their kids these kinds of experiences.

But our children also need to know the value of work. And this is for both our sons and daughters. If you take some moments to read the book of Proverbs, you'll see it's postured as words of wisdom from a father to his child. And one of the themes the Proverbial Father mentions over and over is the indispensable necessity and value of work. The authors warn of the perils awaiting the sloth or lazy person. They plead to not only work hard, but to save, and they speak deeply of the regret awaiting those who exchange the fruits of labor for the comforts of bed. And the book ends by extolling the virtues of a godly woman, who, among other things, works hard. In its broader message of wisdom, then, it is the wise person who understands and commits themselves to the value of work.

When our children turn fifteen and start thinking about getting their driver's permit, I make them a deal. I tell them I will buy them a car and pay the insurance on one condition—they have to secure a job first. How else will they pay for gas? I'm not going to pay for it. Let's just say I've never had to get on my kids about getting a job. And once they secure a job, Korie and I make sure they have a budget where they are saving a minimum of 10 percent, and giving a minimum of 10 percent to the Lord.

A few months into driving, my oldest hit a car—and not just any car, but one belonging to a member of our church. When he told us what happened, we made sure he was okay and then inspected the car, which had been dented pretty significantly. I told him to take it to the auto body shop around the corner, where they said the repair would cost $1,300.

"So, Dad, I need $1,300," my son said. To which I replied, "You've got a savings account." He wasn't too thrilled with me as he felt the pain of digging into his hard-earned savings to pay the bill. Not long after paying the bill, we noticed he had taken on more hours at work, volunteering to pick up extra shifts. When I asked him why, he said he didn't like his savings account being so low, plus he was going off to college and wanted to make sure he had enough money to spend.

Dads, our kids are a lot more resilient than we think. Sadly, neither we nor our children will discover this well of resiliency if we don't put them in positions where they have to dig deep to find it. Let's go to war with entitlement by exposing them to environments outside of their norm, and instilling a work ethic in them.

Chapter 16

BEING A DAD IS
FOR GROWN-UPS

In my opinion, few things in life are more frustrating than opening a Chistmas gift that requires assembly, following the instructions carefully, and then discovering at the end that one of the parts was missing, making the product unable to function properly. So we take the incomplete item back to the store the next day and exchange it for one that is whole.

We may feel a similar frustration when it comes to parenting. While no dad will say he followed God's directions precisely when it comes to raising his kids, we all know the frustration of doing the best we can and then wondering why our child hasn't "turned out right." But unlike the random store product that just so happens to have something missing, *every* child, *every* person, is born with something absent.

The French mathematician and philosopher, Blaise Pascal once observed how all of us try to satisfy our longing for God with things other than God.[1] Sin has gaped an abyss in all of our souls, catapulting humanity to certain "stores" looking for fulfillment. Some of us seek to fulfill the abyss in our souls with alcohol, others with approval from people, others with success and achievement, and still others with money and possessions. These are just a few of what the Bible refers to as idols. And because this hole in our soul is a part of our spiritual DNA, we can parent the best we can and watch as our children go through seasons searching for fulfillment outside of Christ.

Oh yes, Crawford Loritts has been there. And so have I.

It's been said that you'll only be as happy as your unhappiest child. It's not right, but it's true. As our kids have gotten older, we've watched them make some unfortunate choices, choices that inflicted deep pain on Korie and me, causing us to wonder where we went wrong as parents.

Pastor Bryan Loritts, author of a book on fathering, has had kids get suspended from school, sneak out of the home, drink alcohol way before the legal age, and even experiment with drugs. One of our children in particular seemed to have taken out a five-year mortgage on a home in the "far country." And what they don't tell you about children who live in rebellion is the havoc it causes on the marriage. The stress was through the roof. There were times when I yelled. There were times when Korie yelled at me for yelling at our son. I was being too hard, she thought. After all, if God's kindness leads to repentance (Rom. 2:4), shouldn't we try to be kind by overlooking the lying and disrespect? I fired right back with a Romans grenade of my own: "Are we to continue in sin that grace may abound? By no means!" (Rom. 6:1–2). Let's just say that didn't help.

Finally, in what was becoming a far too frequent battle with our son, where I took his phone and privileges away (again), he exhaled, "Don't you see? What you're doing is not working." I had to admit he was right. We had to change our approach, and the answer surprisingly came from my Romans 2:4 wife. She said it was time to give him a wake-up-call experience. He needed to go away, out of state, to a school that would help address the deep issues in his heart, Korie reasoned. Now I had turned into the softie.

So we did some research, and landed on a school well over a thousand miles from home. Around this time, I found myself on yet another airplane headed off to preach to people about how Jesus is better than everything else, while I peered out the window into the early morning light feeling as if Jesus wasn't better in our home. Waves of guilt washed over me. It's one thing to admit we have a hole in the soul and quite another to wonder whether I, through my own brokenness as a parent, had contributed to the widening wound in my son. I started to form a mental list of all that I had done wrong: traveled too much, yelled too much, took things away from him too much, always assumed he was lying. At the end of the list, I was forced to render a verdict of guilty on myself. If only I had been there more, encouraged more, helped out more, hugged more, played with him more ...

By the time I landed, I turned on my phone and began the process of calling home to tell Korie we needed to hold off on the whole out-of-state school thing. I needed to work more on being his friend. But I stopped. I had this overwhelming sense of God telling me, "I've got him. Trust Me with him. Right now he needs you to be a dad, not his friend."

Being a dad, being the *RITE* kind of dad, is for grown-ups. I felt this when we took him out to dinner and affirmed him of our love for him as we recounted our journey together and informed him of our decision. The tears in his eyes staggered me. His pleadings almost broke me. Our drive back to the hotel from his faraway school where we had just dropped him off was filled with the language of tears.

Still feeling like a failure some days later, and reeling from having to say goodbye to one of our sons, I was sitting by myself in the green room of a church between services. There was a knock on the door, and in walked an elderly gentleman who had been at the first service. There was a look of urgency on his face, like he was there to not just shoot the breeze with me, but was on assignment. "I feel deeply as if the Lord wants me to help you with something," he said. Korie and I had been talking about how we were going to pay this tuition. Knowing what God said to me ("I got him"), I told her we were going to trust God. So I opened up and told this gentleman about our need. He nodded his head, encouraged me, and left. Every single month for the next two years, he sent us a check for our son's tuition. When we would get those checks, I would look at them as if they were rainbows—little glorious affirmations of God's promises, His "I got him" promises.

I often think of the statement my father quotes frequently about parenting: "We parents tend to take too much credit when our kids turn out 'right,' and too much blame when they don't." You may know the frustration of parenting with the best of intentions, only to see your kids take tours of duty in the land of rebellion. Maybe you did your best to "keep your daughter off the pole"—you took her out on dates, talked to her about purity, and even gave her a promise ring with which she made a commitment not to have sex until her wedding night, only to discover she's been sleeping around. Or perhaps your son is ensnared in some addiction, and you're watching his life spiral out of control. You've tried everything you can think of to help him, and you're at your very end. Or maybe you just don't like your child. It's hard to put your finger on the one thing about him, but he just doesn't seem to be a very good and kind person. Perhaps he's disrespectful to you and his mom. He lies all the time, and it takes everything in you just to enjoy being around him. It sounds weird, I know, but I've sat with many dads who've made this closeted confession. And in all these cases and more, many dads admit that while they are not perfect, they've done the best they could with what they've had and still have come up short.

Take heart, you're not alone. I often wonder whether God meets the qualifications for being an elder. One of the requirements is the ability to manage his household well. Have you seen God's kids lately? They can be terribly unruly. God referred to Israel as being stiff necked and playing the whore. Like my son, God's son Jonah ran away from Him. His daughter Miriam acted out in racist ways toward Moses's black wife. Moses murdered.

David couldn't leave the ladies alone. If you're looking at your kids and feeling like you're a fathering failure, remember that having unruly kids is not necessarily the sign of parental failure. We have a God who can more than one-up us with stories of rebellious children.

Look closely at how God dealt with his rebellious children. Many times, He gave them hard-to-go-through experiences in order to transform them. Jonah encountered a storm and entered the belly of a great fish. Miriam was struck with leprosy. Israel wandered in a desert. Samson ended up blind and in chains. Surely, these weren't pleasant scenarios for God to watch. And while God certainly relates to us as a friend, there are plenty of moments when He needs to be more of a dad than a friend.

As your kids get older, it would be great to transition into friendship. Even then, there will be times when they will need you to take off your friend hat and give them some experiences they may not like for the greater good of turning their lives around.

Grown-up dads set boundaries—lines in the sand that if crossed yield consequences. One of these lines should be disrespect. I do think children should communicate what they are feeling, but it should be expressed in a certain way. The Bible talks about speaking truth in love, and being kind. God so cherished children respecting their parents that He etched it into stone for all of history when he commanded children to honor their parents. Laced within the notion of honor is respect.

My sons will tell you that while I'm "pretty chill," I can get upset when I hear them disrespecting not just their mother but my wife. Dads, if you have boys, you need to train them to respect women. And if you have daughters, they also need to be committed to respect. While respect in general is a sign of a maturing and decent human being, if your daughters get married it is especially useful, since they are commanded in the Scriptures to respect their husbands. That training should begin now in your home. Respect is a hard line in the sand that needs to be drawn.

Of course, there are other boundaries like being grateful, a team player, humble, and a person of truth—to name only a few. As my father used to say to us, "If you tell a lie, make it your best." He was being somewhat sarcastic, but his point was that if he found out we were lying, we could expect dire consequences. Truth matters.

Dads, sometimes we draw lines that don't need to be drawn. Sometimes we just have to bite our tongues and keep quiet. When one of my sons came home from college with a tattoo, along with earrings and hair that I am convinced would bar him from any respectable job, I sensed God whisper to me, "Keep quiet." Personal preferences do not always equate healthy boundaries. In fact, when Paul warns of fathers not exasperating their children, I think he's alluding to the notion of allowing lesser issues to be made primary ones. Not everything needs to be addressed. Sometimes the best parenting happens when we bite our tongues—really hard.

And when we find our children cross our lines not only repeatedly but also with no remorse or repentance, we have to be prepared to respond. In looking over our journey with our one son, Korie and I have found three things to be vital to his transformation.

First, Korie and I committed ourselves to diligent, warlike prayer. Dads, the best parenting we will ever do is from our knees. My prayer journal is filled with pages dedicated to this one particular son, where I have written out verses to match his needs, and I would spend large amounts of time calling out these verses over him—for years. His turnaround happened after prayer.

Second, when Korie and I were yelling at each other and him, we turned to mentors and friends who had gone down a similar path. The Bible talks about how there's wisdom in a multitude of counselors. As I would confide in some trusted spiritual leaders about our experiences, I was shocked to discover the overwhelming majority of them had gone through the same thing. I sometimes feel as if the church is one big Instagram page where we only testify about the great things God is doing, and leave out the pain, frustration, and not-so-pretty moments. So when Korie and I were at our wits' end, our feeling of failure was only exacerbated by this perception that we were the only ones experiencing such a problem. The truth is we were not the only ones, and we found great solace in hearing from others on a similar path.

Third, Korie and I have given our children hard experiences that would not crush them and actually serve as a catalyst to their development. We implemented this third element after several years of prayer, pleading and seeking other avenues of correction. Finally, through prayer and leaning into wise counsel, and over a whole lot of time when our son was given numerous opportunities to repent, we came to the conclusion that it was time for him to be in another environment, one better equipped to speak to the deep pain in his heart. This is where I had to be an adult and do something I didn't want to do, even though I was convinced I had to do it. In hindsight, I am so thankful God gave me the courage, because what He did in our son continues to amaze us.

About two months after my son graduated from his faraway school, I found myself preaching in Las Vegas. After the service, I was down front shaking hands when out of the corner of my eye I noticed a young man lingering, letting other people slip in front of him to greet me. Finally, when it was his turn to shake my hand, he said, "Loritts? Is that your last name, sir?" I nodded. He then asked, "Do you have a son named _____?" I smiled and nodded again. "Well, I just want to tell you I've really struggled with addiction and ended up in the same school as him. Your son has had a deep influence on my life. In fact, sir, I wouldn't be here in church tonight if it wasn't for him."

I was immediately shocked. Later, I cried. Turning the conversation with this young man over in my mind as I lay in bed that evening, I heard God affirm, "I told you. I've got him."

Failure and fathering go hand in hand. You will blow it even when you had the best of intentions. And while fairy-tale endings are for Hollywood, trust God with your child. Parent from your knees. And when it's time to step up, be a dad and give your kids hard experiences with their good in mind. May God give you the courage to do so.

Chapter 17

THE PLATE

I know a man whose dad was not afraid of handing his children hard experiences. When he and his sisters graduated high school, a big party was thrown at their home, and sometime in the middle of the festivities, they were summoned outside for a private moment with their father. The sight was more than curious: Dad standing on their brick patio, tears streaming down his face while holding a set of fine china. He was crying because he knew the time had come for them to transition into womanhood and manhood. So he would speak words of life and encouragement into their souls. And when he was finished he would thrust the china down onto the brick patio, shattering it into scores of pieces. A moment of silence ensued as they would absorb the shock and stare into this waste of money. Finally, dad breaks the silence by asking, "Do you know what that was? That was your place setting. Off you go out of our home to college (or military, or whatever)." Dad would remind them they could never come back except for visits, while affirming his love for them. Talk about a sobering moment.

This dad's children exude confidence. The word *confidence* comes from the Latin term meaning "with faith." I like that. Faith isn't certainty but presupposes risk, and risk requires resiliency. And where does resiliency emerge? Out of struggle—the kind of struggle imposed upon a person through broken plates on brick patios.

So what became of Paul's son in the faith, Timothy? We know from Scripture that Timothy was not a naturally bold person. He was not the immediate picture of confidence. A good case can be made that he struggled with anxiety. Paul had to remind him to drink a little wine for his stomach issues and frequent infirmities (1 Tim. 5:23). Paul also had to remind Timothy that God had not given him a spirit of fear (2 Tim. 1:7). Timothy was not naturally wired toward acts of courage and steeled confidence. So whatever became of Paul's spiritual son?

As the story goes, Timothy was leading the church in Ephesus when word got around there was a group of people involved in pagan celebrations in his beloved city. Convinced something needed to be done, Timothy went out to confront this crowd of pagans with the truth of God's Word. An argument ensued, a mob was incited, and when the dust settled, Timothy was dead. He was eighty years old, decades removed from his spiritual father, Paul, writing him to have confidence.[1] I can see Paul greeting his son in heaven, showing him the laceration marks on his glorified body that came from his beheading, while Timothy shows him the imprints of stones and fists on his. Both had died with confidence in Jesus Christ. Like father, like son. Dad had made the difference.

The emerging generations of children in the West are suffering from a deficiency of confidence and resilience. It's no coincidence this downturn in what Angela Duckworth calls *Grit* runs on parallel tracks to the uptick in absent dads. If men don't have the confidence to hang in there, why would we expect more from our children?

Dads who make a difference in the lives of their children are those who father with the long view in mind. It's easy as a father to exchange long-term resilience and strength for short-term comfort and happiness. And this is what we do when we do their homework, pay for everything, and blame and berate their coaches and teachers for their lack of playing time and success.

One of my sons had a rough year athletically. For the first time in his life, my son was not starting, and it was his coach's fault— or so he reasoned. He pleaded with me to say something. Now, you should know I would like nothing else than to see my son start every game. And I'd like to believe I can be pretty persuasive when I need to be. After all, I work with words for a living. But I began to think past the season and into the future. Yes, his coach was no walk in the park, but later in life, he'll face bigger challenges from bosses he won't like. What then? He needs to learn to step up now. So I said to him playing time was not my issue, but his. If he wanted to play more, he needed to perform better. My words were almost as shocking to him as my friend's plate smashing was to his kids. But my son stepped up, and toward the end of the season he became a consistent starter.

What's your vision for your children? Maybe things begin with you and your wife taking a weekend away for what one of my mentors calls a "vision trip," when you write down the character traits you want to see in your children. I recommend this list not exceed ten items. You may write things on your list like *grateful* and *hard worker*. After you've compiled your list, craft a plan. When Korie and I talked about wanting children who were grateful, we trained them to say "thank you" to their servers, along with attaching words like "may I" and "please." It was a little rough in the beginning, but over time gratitude was instilled. It all began with a vision and a plan.

Paul had a vision and a plan for Timothy. Paul showed up. When no one else may have believed in Timothy, Paul did. Paul took him under his wing, poured into him, and modeled for Timothy the possibilities of biblical manhood. They walked together in relationship, and Timothy witnessed integrity while ingesting deep biblical teaching. And right as Timothy was getting comfortable with this sedentary lifestyle, Paul gave him vital experiences, shaping him into the man he would become. Ultimately, Paul would place Timothy as the pastor of one of the most strategic cities in the world, while he wrote letters from prison to his son cheering him on, telling him he could do it. What transformed fear-riddled Timothy to a man who boldly took on people walking in darkness? A dad. Dad made all the difference.

And so can you. You don't need to spend a day in seminary,

know a lick of Greek, or have read through the entire Bible to make a tailwind difference in the life of your children. Just show up in *relationship*, *integrity*, *teaching*, and *experience*, trusting God to fill in the gaps. He's doing it for and through me, and I know He'll do it for and through you.

EPILOGUE

E very dad has a set of aspirations for his children, and those aspirations have a basic operating system. Many dads want their kids to be successful by the world's standards—make a lot of money, average the most points on the team, be smart, achieve a certain standard of living, and so on. The desire for success is fueled by the operating system of hard work, so the father drives the child to study harder and practice more in order to achieve at a high level. The problem with success-driven dads is it reduces their children's identity to report cards and stat sheets.

Other dads want their children to be nice, good people, full of character. These dads operate from the principle of moralism, which pretty much links identity and acceptance with the character choices they make as a person. Children of the moralist hear more about being sexually chaste and avoiding drugs and alcohol (to name just a few ideals). The problem with the morals-driven dad is no one ever bats a thousand when it comes to good behavior.

Crawford Loritts was not driven by hard work or moralism, though he did value labor and character. Instead, what fed everything for my father was the good news of being in a relationship with Jesus Christ, or what we would call the gospel. In fact, I believe the best fathering arises out of a gospel-driven operating system. Essentially, this means four things.

The gospel says we are sinners. King David confessed in Psalm 51 how he was born in iniquity and in sin did his mother conceive him (v. 5). Later, Paul would state how all of us have sinned. As one of my friends says, "If sin were blue, we'd all be Smurfs." Sin colors all of who we are.

This understanding of sin is essential to fathering because it sets us on a plane of empathy and understanding when it comes to both our children and ourselves. When I really embrace this idea of sin, I'm not surprised by the lie or laziness or bad decision. In fact, I assume it, and this makes me far more patient as a father, because God is being patient with me. But there's more here. The idea of sin is not just something resident in my children, but it's in me. I think the reason my father was always quick to apologize to us is because he understood what the gospel said was true of him as well—he's a sinner in need of great grace. When we acknowledge that we are fallen, we become humble—and only humble people have the courage to apologize, because they know they are "prone to wander."

Second, the gospel says we are not only sinful, but also deeply loved. As Tim Keller points out, the gospel says we are more sinful than we'd like to admit, yet more loved than we could ever imagine.[1] I don't know where you are with God right now, but

I do know where He is with you: He sees you and your sin, and He loves you, right now, just as you are. He doesn't love what He wants you to become. He doesn't love what He hopes you will be in the future. He loves you right now, no matter what you've done. You may be on your third marriage. You may have children you're estranged from and it's your fault. These things don't affect how much God loves you. He loves you as is, sees you as is, accepts you as is, and wants to save you as is. This is why the Bible says, "God shows his love for us in that *while* we were still sinners, Christ died for us" (Rom. 5:8, emphasis added).

I think God communicates the astounding paradox of the gospel—that we are sinful and loved all at once—through the experience of parenting. I remember holding my children for the first time and being overwhelmed with the thought that I was holding a piece of me, someone I shared DNA with. The connection was indescribable. I look at them all the time and think, "That's me." And then they make bad decisions, talk disrespectfully, or tell the lie, and I am really upset. But I never wish them harm or want to banish them forever. They are both sinful and loved all at once. That's true not just of Quentin, Myles, and Jaden; it's true of all of us—our Father God loves us sinners.

Your addiction won't make God turn His back on you. Your philandering won't make God wash His hands of you. Those moments when you lashed out in abuse may break God's heart, but they don't make Him close the door on you. After all, you've been made in His image, which means there are times God looks at you and says, "That's Me." You are sinful and loved all at once. This is gospel truth.

The third truth of the gospel is that Jesus is God's only means to a relationship with Him. We live in a society where perhaps the worst thing you could be considered is exclusive, but don't we all draw lines where we exclude people? Tolerant people exclude people they think are intolerant. Any group has a set of standards that people have to commit to if they are going to be part of the group. We all have lines. And as we said, good fathering has boundaries. God has one major boundary when it comes to having a relationship with Him—Jesus is the only way. Jesus Himself said this when He remarked, "I am the way, and the truth, and the life; No one comes to the Father except through me" (John 14:6).

God hates sin, yet He loves us. God is committed to justice, and also to grace. So how was our sin going to get dealt with? How were all the addictions, abuse, and lies going to get covered? The answer is Jesus. The death of Jesus satisfied God's just demands for the penalty of your sin and my sin. And it was the death of Jesus that became God's onetime gracious payment to Himself so that you and I don't have to pay.

Remember the story I told earlier of the time my father paid my American Express charges? It was my disobedience against my father that had racked up the debt. American Express couldn't care less about how the charges got there. All they knew was there was a bill that needed to be paid. Dad's payment satisfied the just demands of American Express, and was a deep act of grace on my behalf in which the relationship was restored.

This is what God in Christ has done for us. Dad's decision to pay my debt was informed by the gospel and what Christ did for him on the cross. Dads, when you allow the gospel to seep down into the crevices of your soul, it will push you to radical, insane acts of grace.

Finally, the gospel says my identity is determined not by my performance, but by Christ's performance for me on the cross. The gospel frees me from idolatry. An idol is anything, even a good thing, that becomes an ultimate thing. Idols are things we turn to for meaning, value, and identity. All of us have struggles with idolatry. Even more sobering is that, if you don't parent from a gospel operating system, you will inevitably encourage idolatry in your children.

I see this all the time sitting in the stands with other dads watching our kids play sports. The way we can push our kids to unhealthy extremes, and the impossible standards we hold them to, is idolatry. We are sending the message that they are their performance. It's also true when it comes to academics, and a myriad of other things. Idols are everywhere, and not just on totem poles. They are in our hearts.

Dads who father *RITE*, from a gospel undercurrent, teach their children to put gospel distance between who they are and their report cards, stat sheets, and social media followers. And dads who father *RITE* will mark their kids not just for this life, but for the life to come.

So maybe your journey begins not with a relationship with your children, but with God—the one who created and loves you. Maybe it begins with you confessing your sins, receiving His forgiveness, and inviting Him into relationship with you. If we are going to unleash the power of the gospel in our homes, let it first begin in our hearts.

ACKNOWLEDGMENTS

I feel like this book is one big acknowledgment to my father, Crawford Loritts. When I talked with Moody about wanting to write a book on being a dad, I felt it was really important not to convey these four gifts in didactic form, but rather in a narrative, showing primarily how my dad fathered me. It took years for me to see how truly blessed I am to be his son. Thanks, Dad, for your investment in my life. I am who I am today in large part because of you.

My children, Quentin, Myles, and Jaden, are gifts of grace to me (along with my bride, Korie). They've endured my brokenness and many mistakes, and have allowed me to lead them. I still hold a thread of text messages to one of my sons where I apologized to him for something I should not have done. He simply responded, "I forgive you, and I love you, Dad." Their generosity toward me is what allows me to father them.

Korie has been a huge encouragement to me in my journey as a dad. I can't tell you how many times I've come home from work and she's pulled me to the side and informed me about some issue one of our sons needs to be challenged about; or other times when she has admonished me for my approach or judgment with them. Her gentle words have been so influential.

I'm also honored to continue this work with my agent, Andrew Wolgemuth; assistant, Sharon Ortiz; and the people at Moody Publishers. No one just sits behind a computer and writes a book. Writing is a team sport, and God's surrounded me with an all-star team. A special shout-out goes to Greg Thornton and his great wisdom and encouragement in this project.

Finally, to you dads who are in the journey with me: Our kids will one day leave our homes (we pray!), but we will never stop being their fathers. May God give us wisdom in this lifelong quest.

NOTES

Tailwind Dads

1. I recall H.B. Charles Jr. saying this in a sermon, but I cannot recall which one.

Warrior Dad

1. This section is informed by Ray Vander Laan's "In the Footsteps of the Disciples" lecture tour in Israel.

Chapter 1: Receipts from Dad

1. "Finished a Day of Teaching, 'A Day Wasted,'" *History Tech* (blog), April 12, 2010, https://historytech.wordpress.com/2010/04/12/finished-a-day-of-teaching-a-day-wasted/.

Chatper 5: Letters

1. Peter F. Drucker, *The Effective Executive: The Definitive Guide to Getting the Right Things Done* (New York: Collins, 2006), 26.

Chapter 7: Apologies

1. Peggy Wallace Kennedy, *The Broken Road: George Wallace and a Daughter's Journey to Reconciliation* (New York: Bloomsbury Publishing, 2019), 133.

Chapter 9: Assumptions

1. Mandy Gambrell, "Research Says Cohabitation in the U.S. is Rising, while Marriage is Declining," ABC9, WCPO Cincinnati, March 5, 2019, https://www.wcpo.com/lifestyle/research-says-cohabitation-in-the-u-s-is-rising-while-marriage-is-declining.

Chapter 13: The Airplane

1. Malcolm Gladwell, *Outliers: The Story of Success* (New York: Little, Brown and Company, 2008).

Chapter 14: The Bat

1. I learned this in Ray Vander Laan's "In the Footsteps of the Disciples" lecture tour in Israel.
2. Daniel I. Block, *Judges, Ruth: An Exegetical and Theological Exposition of Holy Scripture* (New American Commentary), (Nashville, TN: Holman Reference, 1999)
3. Robert L. Hubbard, *The Book of Ruth*, New International Commentary on the Old Testament (Grand Rapids: Eerdmans, 1989).

Chapter 16: Being a Dad Is for Grown-Ups

1. Blaise Pascal, *Pensées* (New York: Penguin Books, 1966), 75.

Chapter 17: The Plate

1. John Foxe, *Foxe's Book of Martyrs* (Philadelphia: Claxton, 1881), 20.

Epilogue

1. Timothy Keller with Kathy Keller, *The Meaning of Marriage: Facing the Complexities of Commitment with the Wisdom of God* (New York, Dutton, 2011), 56.

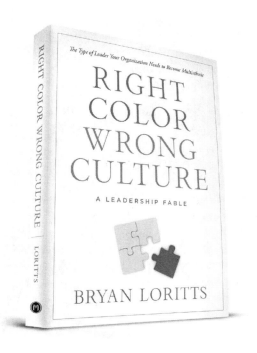

WHO DOES GOD TRUST WITH LEADERSHIP?

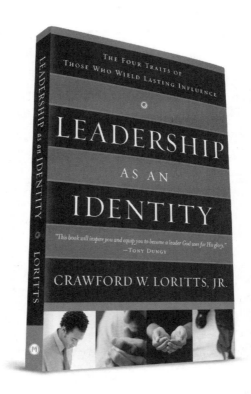